FINDING SUCCESS WITHIN

52 Life Skills For Young Indians

Vivek Atray

First Printing: 2020

Finding Success Within

52 Life Skills For Young Indians

Invincible Publishers

ISBN No. "978-93-89600-35-3"

Invincible Publishers

Registered Address: 201A, SAS Tower, Sector 38, Gurgaon - 122003

Phone - +91-124-4034247, +91 9355675555

www.invinciblepublishers.com

Introduction

It is very difficult to encapsulate all the skills required for living a happy and successful life in one book, but 52 Life Skills for Young Indians is an attempt to do just that. This volume and its contents are universal in applicability and appeal, although written with Indian audiences in mind.

Very few of us are able to accomplish the onerous task of balancing our personal lives and our work, being successful while also being happy, interacting effectively with others and leading a life which inspires us to wake up each morning with zest and zeal.

The skills required for building a successful career and leading a fulfilling life are much the same but there are subtle requirements to both which we often miss.

None of us can lead a cheerful and calm existence given the turbulences that affect us all the time, if we do not keep the bigger picture in mind. And in these technology intensive times, leading a life which focuses on the true meaning of life becomes difficult! The tips given herein are practical and doable. Each of us can attempt to follow them, partly if not in their entirety.

Polishing your edges, sharpening your axe, and keeping the creative flame burning brightly within you will give you immense joy and satisfaction in the years ahead.

Let us then dive deep into these 52 Tips for Young Indians together, and let us see how many of them we can follow and live up to!

Acknowledgements & Gratitude

I'm sharing some thoughts hereunder with a deep sense of gratitude.

The only reason that I have been able to write a book of this magnitude is the magnificent support of my family, friends and well wishers. Not that this is a monumental work in terms of number of words or pages, but it has been a gigantic task for me to write it. I have had to delve deep into whatever expertise, experience and mind space I possess. I have had to ponder deeply over what really makes for a successful and happy life in this ultra-modern era.

With the surge of technology having overtaken most of our hitherto simple activities, the definitions of success and happiness appear to have changed. But have they really? Success without a sense of inner peace and joy has no real meaning. In any case, most worldly achievements are fleeting in nature. It is the calm river of permanent joy flowing beneath the veneer of restlessness which truly gives us the joy we seek.

And that calmness comes from being in the company of those we love. In my case, my wife Neena who has been a beautifully smiling encourager in each moment of my life and endeavours is the paramount force behind my ability to churn out writings like these. She has ever egged me on to do 'more and better' as a writer and motivational speaker.

Our daughters Spriha and Kavya are caring souls and love permeated blessings in human form. Their very presence is enough to inspire the best in me, in my talks, and in my writings. The boundless love of my family has made me what I am, for sure.

Memories of my parents, Rama and JP Atray; of their everlasting goodness, and of my grandparents, have been with me throughout. The sweetness of my sisters, the dazzling twins, Suruchi-Surabhi, their families, and the loving thoughts that keep flowing towards me from my extended family, my in-laws, my amazing friends, my seniors, from past and present, just keep me going, without fatigue, without regret.

My publishers, Invincible, and all those who have contributed their mite to this book, especially Mrs Ramesh Gupta who has translated it into Hindi, deserve my gratitude as well.

Above all, the eternal teachings and divine love of my Guru have emboldened me to just be myself and try to shower happiness wherever I go.

The youth of India inspire me no end. I am forever grateful to them for responding so warmly to my words and thoughts. They need as much guidance and inspiration as they can get from those who have trodden before them along the same pathways. It is my endeavour to ignite the spark within them which has the potential to light up this world of ours in all the right ways.

Vivek Atray

To the memory of my closest friend,
Sunil Sharma, who was verily the ambassador of
happiness.

******

"The laughter of the infinite God must vibrate through your smile. Let the breeze of His love spread your smiles in the hearts of men."
Paramahansa Yogananda,
author of the Autobiography of a Yogi.

Foreword

I am delighted to be writing the foreword of the book *Finding Success Within - 52 Life Skills for Young Indians*, authored by Vivek Atray.

As an ex-bureaucrat, a motivational speaker and an author, Vivek Atray has inspired many, many young people to adopt a positive approach to life.

In his book, *Finding Success Within,* Vivek Atray takes look at some of the recipes for success. He has covered Entrepreneurship and The Winning Habit in a manner that readers would feel motivated to adopt his ideas.

I have always believed that in life, true champions never give up. True leaders do not have any regrets since they have always given their best to everything they do!

Each of us yearns to make a mark in life, and we can do that in every worthwhile pursuit by making an earnest effort without harbouring the fear of failure.

Vivek Atray is a motivational speaker who is working passionately to inculcate the right mindset amongst the youth of today. I am certain that his book *'Finding Success Within'* will spread his message of positivity, calmness and balance, which are the real ingredients for success and happiness.

My best wishes always!

Shiv Khera
Internationally Renowned Speaker and Author of
YOU CAN WIN

Life is not about marks,
it is about making a mark!

Vivek Atray

Contents

Career Skills

Redefining your personality

Creative Skills

Relationships Matter

The Bigger Picture of Life

Career Skills

Skills for the Entire Career

Tip Number 1

Be Enthusiastic Forever

It is an established fact that some amount of passion is necessary to accomplish anything of note. Going through the motions and simply existing is not likely to yield anything of note.

The inner yearning to achieve levels of shine and sparkle is what counts in a career. There are hundreds of thousands of people who simply 'survive', go through the motions, and live a dull, routine life.

But some others are different. I was at Ranchi Airport recently and was served by a young waiter named Umang at a new cafe. There was nothing spectacular about him, and he simply did his job with quiet efficiency, but his demeanour was such that it left a favourable impression upon me.

The first words that Umang said to me were 'Sir, why don't you take this seat here. It has a nicer view.' I nodded and accepted his suggestion, even though I had previously selected another one. He then proceeded to just somehow make me feel really comfortable and I lapped up the warmth that he exuded, as well as his cheerful banter.

It was that little bit of extra effort on his part to be enthusiastic in his approach towards work that made him stand apart. Sometimes that is all we need in order to create an impression-some extra effort and a positive approach.

There is no need to possess a flamboyant personality or brilliant skill sets in order to be noticed; whatever may be your career. By sheer dint of verve and enthusiastic endeavour, you can rise above competition and keep shining.

Your own self esteem and inner poise will improve if you are full of the desire to do more and better!

Actor Anil Kapoor is an example of someone who emanates a sheer sense of joie de vivre all the time. He belies his age and looks ready for action at every moment of his life. It has been his extra verve that has made him stand apart over the years and even propelled him to the pinnacle of the Bollywood rankings at the peak of his career.

When Anil Kapoor started out he was not considered 'star material'. Yet, with his professional approach and his high energy performances he started to impress one and all. He worked hard and catapulted to the top of the ladder riding on his talent and never say die spirit.

There is an indefinable something that separates the real doers from the rest. And that something is surely linked to the additional amount of bubbling energy that they bring to their business or work. It is that surge of extra enthusiasm which will help you to truly succeed in your career.

What you need to do

- You must regularly summon from within a little extra energy in order to find success.
- Avoid dullness and inaction which usually lead to nothingness.
- That additional ounce of "wanting to be the best" can bring about amazing results.
- When you get up each morning, you can be like a hungry lion or like a slender gazelle, but you must be eager to run like hell! Don't rest on your laurels.
- The spirit of seeking to ever improve and wanting to make each day count is what sets apart the true champion from the rest of the pack.

The process of Finding Success Within is the secret to life. Happiness, peace and success can only be found in our own hearts and minds. Instead of searching for them in external conditions we must look deeply within and adopt an attitude of gratitude as well as positivity, above all else!

Vivek Atray

Tip Number 2

Strive Hard with a Focussed Approach

A story goes like this: A busy gentleman arrived at an airport, summoned a cab, and told the driver, 'Please drive as fast as you can!'

After about 20 minutes of fiddling frantically with his phone and reading important papers for the meeting that he was scheduled to attend, the gentleman realised that the taxi was headed in the wrong direction.

He promptly admonished the driver. 'Where are you going, driver? This is the wrong way!' The driver responded somewhat sardonically. 'Sir you just said drive as fast as you can. You never told me where to go. I thought maybe some anti social elements were chasing you or something, and you just wanted to escape!'

Direction and purpose are so very important in life. Very often our focus is scattered and so we are striving hard for a valid objective is absolutely required. But to go a mad in the pursuit of scoring a goal is not sensible at all. The goal post may have shifted several times while we were busy preparing to shoot! We have to reorient ourselves whenever needed.

We have to search deep inside with a focussed mindset for the direction towards which we want to head. Hard work certainly pays but not if we keep slogging without focussing. Equally importantly, one should cut out unnecessary activities that eat into one's regular schedule. Prioritisation leads to quicker and sustained progress towards one's real goals. Dissipation of our energy and effort in non-productive directions has to be checked and stemmed at the earliest.

A woodcutter was once told that he could cut as much wood as his strength permitted; all the wood that he would cut by the end of that day would be his.

He began the day with feverish energy and almost maniacally. By 4 pm he was absolutely famished and fatigued. His axe was blunt and his efficiency was poor.

A well meaning passer-by observed his plight and advised him to take a break, as also to sharpen his axe. But the woodcutter was obsessed with his mindless frenzy and simply refused to listen. Very soon he collapsed and had to be rushed to a doctor by the same well-wisher!

The lesson to be learnt is that we must not direct our efforts at unattainable or ill conceived goals. We have to take a reality check from time to time, re-focus if necessary, and channelize our energies towards objectives which are commensurate with our real goals.

Nalin Sharma was a high profile executive in a foreign embassy in New Delhi. He was also pursuing a doctorate in international relations, his chosen field of study in life.

But the number of invitations he received every week for social and networking dinners kept mounting. The price of his popularity was that he had little time to spend with his family. His research work was totally pushed to the background, and two years passed without any progress. He put on a lot of weight since he was eating out every day,and he always looked stressed out. He never had the heart to say 'No' to anyone who invited him. He had thought that by attending each such networking event he would really further his career prospects. Little did he realise that he would lose both his peace of mind and his health. He pondered over his situation and realised that he had lost the balance of his life by overdoing things.

Having learnt his lesson, he spent the next few months focussing on what really mattered to him- his core work, his fitness and his doctoral degree. Nalin's life was soon back on track thereafter. By correcting the course of his life and re-focussing on the real priorities, he surged ahead.

What you need to do

- Dynamic action in the direction of your overall aims is much needed and desirable.
- Avoid continuous mindless activity. If you do not channelize your energy towards your goals, your efforts will be counter productive.
- Reassess the direction in which you are applying your energies on weekly basis, and re-focus or re- orient them if you have to.

Tip Number 3
Choosing a Career that You Love

Mansi, a qualified Chartered Accountant in Mumbai had a comfortable corporate job. But right from her student days she had never really loved financial analysis, nor was she fond of number crunching. Her family had a long history of producing Chartered Accountants, and she had followed the family tradition, despite not really wanting to.

Then one day, on a long solo walk by the Marine Drive she thought deeply about her career and where it was headed. She realised that she had no desire to sit before computers all her life. She wanted to pursue her passion for creative writing. That evening she made a life changing decision.

In the next three years, bit by bit, she built up her skill and confidence as a writer and actually published three novels. She also ventured into content writing and did well enough to be able to say good bye to the profession of accounting!

Life is not meant to be lived in a state of denial. Nor is it to be lived in an environment of perennial discomfort. One has to be at ease with one's career and life situation. Of course we have to make the best of what we have and try to succeed in every venture towards our goals.

However one has to endeavour to find a career that gives joy and produces enthusiasm within. Agreed, it is well nigh impossible for each young lad to become an Indian cricketer and for each young girl to become a world badminton champion. It is not possible for every IAS aspirant to successfully qualify for the premier service.

Yes, these are career choices that many people would want to make, but few can attain. However, what can be ensured is that you enjoy your work to the extent possible. And for that purpose you have to make the best of what you have.

But the attempt must be to enter a career that is as close to one's heart as is plausible.

An example of achieving just that can be found in the life of Rohit Singh of New Delhi. Rohit always wanted to be a doctor and he tried hard to enter a medical college but could not succeed in his attempt. He felt downcast for several years. He had to take up sundry jobs such as that of a salesman and a medical representative.

A chance encounter with a lesser known magazine found him gazing at a recruitment advertisement for a post of Hospital Administrator. He enrolled for a one year programme in that field and thereafter ended up heading the administration of a medium sized hospital, due to his newly acquired expertise.

By working in a hospital and serving mankind in his own way, Rohit achieved his ambition of serving the medical profession, even if not as a doctor!

There are several twists and turns in life, all along the road. Life does not entail linear progression. One has to go through several meandering paths to reach one's goals.

We must not worry too much about short term results and setbacks. You must try to choose a career option of your liking and get into the best possible role within it. But if things do not seem to be working out, there are possibilities today that enable us to change our work profile relatively easily. And we must do so when the need arises.

Career Changes:

There are people who spend long portions of their careers in situations where they hate their work days. They have to put up with great discomfort since they hardly enjoy even a single moment at office. If this is the case with you, then you will burnout very soon.

You have to take the plunge! Career changes can be of many kinds. People switch from private jobs to setting up entrepreneurial ventures. Some people do the reverse! There are also some like yours truly who quit government service to take up creative assignments or activities. I quit the service after 25 years for the sake of pursuing my passion for motivational speaking and writing. And not a single day has passed since then, when I have regretted my decision.

Yet one has to be meticulously prepared with various options before planning such a move. There is no point in regretting it later because of lack of preparation.

Career changes or not, you must analyse the trend of one's career and endeavour to find the option which makes your heart sing, if not bounce.

What you need to do

- You have to ensure that you do not get into a career which makes you uncomfortable. There is no point in spending years feeling terrible about the job you are in.
- When so much time and energy is to be spent at work, why not try your hardest to move closer to your true calling? Review your work life periodically and ask yourself whether your work is in the realm that you really prefer.
- Choosing and settling into a profession that you love or at least, like, is vital!
- If you have to change your career because your priorities or tastes have changed over the years, do not dither. Plan properly and make the change.

Tip Number 4:
The Ingredients for Being an All-Rounder

A uni-dimensional approach will not lead to a fulfilling life. By filling your mind and thoughts with just one type of activity you are unable to realise your true potential as a creative human being.

If your work involves financial analysis and you are good at your work, you will do even better by learning the salsa dance on Sundays! Or by taking up a cookery course. Or by indulging in nature photography at times.

When you go to work on Monday morning, you should be fresh and ready for action. And your mind cannot be fresh if you have been mulling over some financial analysis all weekend long.

A different part of the brain, the right brain, has to be used for creative pursuits and therefore it is a good idea to learn something totally new and distinct from your own field.

Gardening, nature walks, photography, playing musical instruments, writing poetry or badminton; anything that is refreshingly distinct and also gives enjoyment to you from within is worth endeavouring to learn.

A great example is someone like Sundar Pichai who is a life all-rounder in the truest sense. Having risen from humble origins at his home town Madurai, he scaled the heights of the corporate world to become the CEO of Google. But his childhood fondness for cricket never paled and he has often declared publically that he would have loved to be an Indian cricketer!

His idols were and are Sunil Gavaskar and Sachin Tendulkar, as they are for many of us. Pichai obviously transports the excitement of cricket into his work life as well.

This multidimensional approach to life, with multiple interests and pursuits is probably the foremost way to live and succeed.

In any case this is the era of diversity, of widespread knowledge and multifarious types of opportunities. No one can remain in his work cocoon.

You should try and find something else that excites you apart from your work, something that makes you feel invigorated and makes you bring out a special aspect of your persona.

There are people who discover talents hidden deep within themselves later in life. They never knew that such qualities existed in them.

Believe it or not, the Chancellor of a popular University in North India is learning Chinese these days, and has recently learnt how to play the drums. He performs regularly on stage at campus events which have a musical requirement!

The emphasis in this chapter is on creativity outside your work. Of course you can and must be creative at work too. Being of creative mindset at large will always make you shine. Take that creative spirit with you into all your activities, official and personal.

What you need to do

- You need to think differently, find creative outlets that interest you.
- Music, writing, art, sports, photography anything that makes your heart sing must become a part of your life in a big way.
- You need not excel at such creative pursuits but you

certainly need to indulge in them frequently, to get your mind off work and to use a different part of your brain.

- Pick up the gauntlet and go for it! You must act as soon as possible and start that tennis lesson or guitar class once you have chosen your passion.
- Also become an all rounder by taking interest in other people, other cultures, other countries. Do not stagnate in your own eco-system without being aware of what is going on in the outside world.

Tip Number 5:
Prioritising- Knowing What Really Matters!

We spend a large part of our lives indulging in activities that are rather unproductive and do not represent either work or entertainment or creativity.

Agreed, there are several compulsions which keep us busy most of the time. But there are many avoidable time consumers which need not get the attention they do from us.

A case in point is a typical government official. He or she would necessarily have to attend many meetings which hardly seem like coming to an end. An official in India would also usually have to undertake several tasks which are not a part of his duty and which are just time-eaters!

Mohit Gupta found this out to his chagrin when he joined a premier state service. He was unable to focus on substantive work during his early career, and spent hours each week attending only to coordination related tasks or public dealing. Yes, these do form an important aspect of any government functionary's ambit, but the real focus of governance has to be on planning, strategy, innovation and service delivery.

A few years later Mohit found the situation becoming even more untenable. He was posted in some truly meaningful departments like agriculture and industries, but he was unable to make a mark. He seemed to be fire-fighting all the time!

Mohit spent long hours in office and his family felt neglected. And though he won intermittent praise for his diligent work from his superiors and peers, he always felt that 'something' was missing!

A much awaited holiday at a beach destination made him realise that he could offer much more to the world if he was not shackled by the system he was a part of.

His family supported him and he took the plunge, by resigning and joining an NGO as its chief executive.

He dedicated himself to the organised welfare of large numbers of street children, something he loved doing.

Mohit's wife and children immediately felt that their lives had been elevated to another level as he was able to spend quality time with them now. He also appeared more calm and cheerful as against the irritable Mohit that he used to be.

There are many Mohits and also Malinis out there who are unable to extricate themselves from work- life imbalance. They carry on for years in relative drudgery. And they need not be from the government sector. They could be anywhere, doing anything, but deep down in their hearts they know that they are uncomfortable in their present situations.

Each of them needs to assess periodically the direction in which their lives are headed. They need to see the bigger picture of their lives, and whether their families and loved ones are getting enough of them.

Prioritising also means that one chooses quality over quantity. We need to analyse our days, weeks, months and years. We need to examine whether we are devoting enough of our energy and time to the 'real thing'!

In my view, family and loved ones come on top of the priority list, followed by work and creative interests. Then come socialising and leisure. Last on the list are needless pursuits- 'must-dos' which are often actually 'must-not-dos'!

All of these are important in their own way, but our lives should revolve more around the real priorities of life, not the forced ones.

What you need to do

- Assess your routine and mentally analyse what you are focussing your time and energy upon. This would enable you to make corrections and improvements.

- Prioritisation is a must if you are to lead a productive and creative life. The sooner you take decisions necessary to reorient your life in accordance with your priorities, even if they are tough ones, the better your life will become!

- Make up your mind to minimise time wastage and do not succumb to social compulsions more than is necessary.

Refining your Professional Persona

Tip Number 6:

Polishing the Edges: Honing Your Personality!

Lt. Gen. JFR Jacob, a decorated soldier and former Governor of Punjab recognised the need for each individual to polish himself adequately in today's world. "It is not the survival of the fittest but the survival of the slickest!" he said emphatically to me one day, during a discussion on Chandigarh city's Tourism and IT promotion plans.

Today there is more communication, more commercialisation, more frenzied activity in the world than ever before in the history of our planet.

And this gigantic global roller coaster requires us to be sharp and on the ball, at the ready always, ever prepared to put our best foot forward.

Gone are the days when one could get away with being slipshod, lazy and ungainly.

Random people who frequent a glitzy Shopping Centre in India's metropolitan cities could easily pass off as fashion models these days. Many of them!

That is not to say that we should ape them or keep trying to look glamorous all the time, but possessing a pleasing persona and being smartly dressed for any occasion are given requirements these days.

Developing a personality that appeals to onlookers, even if it does not bowl them over, is almost our duty these days. Facial features have nothing to do with this.

Physical fitness and constant exercise as well as a cheerful attitude add volumes to a personality. If one feels awkward and inadequate in one's growing up years, it is quite natural to feel so. But there are ways in which one can work at building up one's confidence and communication skills.

Physical grooming is also a requirement these days though there is no necessity to splurge money on beauty treatments and expensive hairdos unless one has the money, time and inclination to do so!

In the English classic, My Fair Lady, a very raw young woman portrayed by the charming Audrey Hepburn undergoes accent and pronunciation training under the guidance of two venerable gentlemen. She transforms herself into a swan-like lady with all her Ps and Qs in order within a matter of a few weeks.

Most people in this world can learn to speak fluently and look stylish with some effort. There are of course personality development programmes available in every neighbourhood these days. Image management consultants are also doing rather well.

***Public Speaking Skills*:** Speaking skills can be developed by practising in front of small groups of friends or even your own siblings. Five minute speeches on any given topic can do wonders to building your confidence. To be able to speak with confidence in a group of people, or hold your own in a discussion with 'smart' people, you have to practice repeatedly the art of speaking with confidence. There is no short cut for this.

Pronounciation and vocabulary are secondary qualities when compared to clarity and cheerfulness while addressing audiences. An inner calm will reflect in your personality and impress one and all.

Having conducted several sessions on public speaking skills, I am aware of the trepidation and nervousness that many people feel about speaking on stage. But focussed training and a little practice can make an average speaker into a great one.

Being stylish also means being comfortable in your own skin, with your own self. There is no need to start aping someone else and trying to become someone totally different.

The best way is to refine your own qualities of communication and your own appearance gradually. Everyone can attain an impressive personality which makes people admire us, and which boosts our own confidence.

What you need to do

- Becoming an individual with a persona to admire is not everybody's cup of tea, but it is possible to refine a personality, bit by bit.
- By analysing your weaknesses and gradually carrying out whatever improvements are possible, you can really transform yourself.
- It is possible to completely overhaul your personality by developing inner confidence, learning to speak smartly, and removing some chinks in your armour, or rough edges in your persona.
- Practise public speaking repeatedly. It is important to be able to speak well and with clarity in today's era.

Tip Number 7:
Keep Sharpening Your Career Skills

Times are changing very fast in the present era. Every facet of society keeps innovating itself constantly.

In such a scenario you not only have to keep pace with ongoing developments, but you also have to beat the rest of the pack.

Sharpening your skills will always stand you in good stead. Even if you have to take a break from work and hone those inner talents once in a while, you must go ahead.

The woodcutter's story in Chapter 2 is a prime example of how you need to distance ourselves from your work life scenario, in order to gain a better perspective and understand what you need to do to keep improving your skills and performance.

The process of upgrading your career skills should be a life-long, never ending one. There is always something new to pick up.

This could be some new software that eases your own profile management. It could be a search engine optimisation technique that has been developed recently. Or it could be a learning trend that has taken on global proportions. An example of the latter is what has come to be known as Blended Learning. This is especially of use to school teachers, but also to any professional who is into training or class room activity, at an institute level or at the corporate level.

The whole world is grappling with the dilemma of how much technology and artificial intelligence to allow into the classroom. And those who understand such trends are able to keep pace with the global preferences on the matter.

They realise that it is best to adopt new technology to bring about optimum results, while ensuring that traditionally proven methods are not dispensed with, unnecessarily.

A new skill or a new fangled way of doing things thus becomes a friend to the innovatively minded, receptive professional.

By reading up on such a trend, a professional can expound his new found insight in group discussions and impress at senior level meetings. You are then noticed by those who matter and are more likely to scale the ladder of success.

Ingraining new skills or knowledge is of course not only about making an impression on others. It is about utilising your skill and knowledge pool to truly make a mark in your career.

Those who rest on their laurels, stagnate in the long run. You may have been a topper in college but if you have not read anything worthwhile in the past ten years, you have not kept pace with the rest of the world.

It is truly important to learn from others all the time. To pick up new ways of doing things, and new skills, is a great idea. By going back to the drawing board, and by refreshing your memory you energise yourself at all times along your journey.

An example of someone who just kept trying to learn new skills is a former Mathematics Professor, who launched coaching classes, then a group of colleges and ultimately a University.

What's more, he is learning Chinese these days as a 70 year old! He is believed to be the topper of his class. And to top all that, he has recently learnt how to play the drums! He actually plays them at University level functions even though he is the Chancellor!

If a 70 year old can reinvent himself in amazing ways like these, you and I can certainly continue to renew ourselves every year, and become superior versions of our own selves in the process.

What you need to do

- The idea is to be able to renew your skills continually.
- You have to maintain that inner eagerness to enhance and uplift your knowledge and skills by continually reading and learning.
- The more you remain open to learning new skills and absorbing new ideas, the more successful your career will be.
- Attending a mid career course or taking time off to read extensively and/or learn new tricks of your trade, online or offline, is always a great idea.

Being an excellent communicator

Tip Number 8:

Communicating Effectively and Precisely

One of the most under rated factors that influences success is the ability or lack of it to communicate with precision and exactitude. Even more significant than the science of communication is its art. A natural communicator will garner a lot of good will and popularity, as well as career fillips in various ways.

What immediately sets a professional apart from everyone else is the set of communication skills that he or she brings out when it matters. Good looks do not matter after their initial 'shock and awe' value!

The capability of speaking lucidly and even charmingly is a true winner.

I was once posted as Sub Divisional Magistrate of Kalka sub division in the foothills of the Himalayas. A leading politician decided to make village visits to hear about the woes and aspirations of the general populace.

At one of the villages where the said politician's cavalcade halted, with officers like me in tow, we found a tall gangling member of the village panchayat speaking forcefully against the State Government. He all but blasted the powers that be, in a short but powerful speech which left all present quite stunned. He was so sure of what he said, and so voluble, that he simply bowled the audience over and got them cheering. When the man spoke against the visiting politician, who sat right before him, perched on a specially provided charpoy the cheers were especially loud!

The political 'leader' was soon quite on the back foot. He gently mouthed his remonstrations not wanting to annoy the villagers, but denying all the allegations.

But what came as an utter shock to me was the following suggestion that the said political figure whispered into my ear

"I will request the Government to appoint this man as a member of the area Agriculture Marketing committee. That should win him over and bring over him to my fold!"

And sure enough, after a few weeks the said village denizen was allotted not only a position but also an official vehicle by the State. And primarily because he spoke up to be noticed when it really mattered!

Each one of us does not have to indulge in similar opportunism to rise in life, but it is clear that we do have to speak up when it matters, and speak well!

Even more of an asset is the ability to be effective in communicating on a day to day basis. A leader needs to convey clear and precise messages to his team, orally and in writing. He or she needs to make sure that there is no lack of clarity on account of inefficient communication.

Email writing is a tricky task too, for many people. Even sending text messages becomes a challenge for some. It is imperative to ensure that basic writing skills are a part of your repertoire. Add to that the ability to send lucid and unambiguous messages.

Even at a personal level, you need to ensure that you are not misunderstood by those who really matter. There is no point in keeping silent when it would be better to share what is on your mind. And there is equally no sense in blurting out something which might hurt your loved ones!

What you need to do

- If you lack oral or written skills you must work on them and improve steadily. The idea is not to have an extensive vocabulary, but the ability to communicate with clarity and precision.

- By being an effective communicator, even if that talent has to be acquired, a professional can scale several peaks and even win some hearts along the way.
- The habit of constantly communicating with those in your professional or personal circle will make you popular as well as successful.
- Don't hold back when you feel the slightest need to communicate. But be discerning about what to say, how and when!

Tip Number 9:
Presentation Skills- The Slicker The Better

The need of the hour in today's era is to be able to efficiently put across ideas that you have come up with. The audience or the group to whom a Power Point Presentation or PPT is being delivered will always appreciate a slick and smart presentation as opposed to a long drawn and boring one.

To deliver a good presentation, you can follow these 4 C's- confidence, calmness, clarity and conciseness.

Too many slides and too much text on them is never a great idea. What you need to do is to cover all the points without writing too much about them, and without repeating them.

To start with, giving an overview of your presentation is a good idea. This should be followed by a few slides for each topic, with minimum necessary comments, which have to be incisive and impactful. A well worded conclusion to end the presentation would be the icing on the cake. Using simple colours and fonts is a good idea. Pictures should not be overdone, though some visuals are usually required. Videos, if any, should be brief and relevant. Many presenters use long videos and focus on entertaining their audiences a great deal more than needed!

Hyperlinks should be used if needed, but not too many.

Making a PPT too elaborate by displaying large amounts of data is an avoidable practice, unless absolutely essential.

Too many statistical tables are always a burden on the mind of the viewers.

There are some people who go on and on with their PPTs. They bore the onlookers to death and whatever they sought to achieve through the PPT goes out of the window!

In private companies this happens at times but in government departments this is especially a worry. So much so that a very enlightened Chief Secretary of a northern state actually declared that no PPT would be delivered for a period longer than 12 minutes! The resultant time-saving can well be imagined, as well as the lessening of the ordeal to which officials were hitherto subjected!

One must also realise the difference and similarity between an extempore speech and a PPT. The main difference is that in the case of a PPT the audience spends more time reading and gazing at the screen; there is more detail, and there are pictures that explain a lot immediately. In an extempore speech the speaker has the undivided attention of the viewers and can make more of an impact with his or her persona.

Some people feel more comfortable with a PPT as they feel a little less nervous and ‘lean’ or depend on the slides quite a lot! That’s fine, but even they should be able to make an impact by the power of the spoken word. The way they stand, the manner in which they use voice intonation, and the skill with which they convince their audience of the idea they have, is what will matter.

It is also possible and necessary to distribute handouts at times. These could contain printed copies of the PPT or a gist there of. The trick is to ensure that the group does not keep reading the printed literature at the cost of paying attention to the presenter.

By using witty one-liners it is possible to keep the audience in a receptive and peppy mood. The speaker must not plunge into drabness and dullness. Making cheerful comments at the beginning and the conclusion as well as the use of intermittent humour is a great way to make a presentation.

What you need to do

- The secret to being an able presenter is to follow these 4 C's- confidence, calmness, clarity and conciseness. If you keep these 4 C's of presenting in mind, you will never go wrong.
- Practice your presentation before you actually deliver it; see how much time it takes, and make sure it flows well.
- Do not make the presentation too long or too brief. Use handouts where necessary.
- Make sure your delivery is crisp and to the point, and your manner pleasing to your audience.

Tip Number 10:
Writing Skills- Reports, Email and Texting

A good communicator will be precise and correct in his or her written messages. There is no scope for technology related gaffes which the 'Autocorrect' feature seems to throw up these days! There is also no scope for misspelling someone's name or getting a designation wrong. One has to be exact while sending out letters or emails.

We often tend to take our spelling errors and grammatical mistakes with a pinch of salt, and a 'chalta-hai' kind of attitude. But it is highly likely that a shoddily written email with a plethora of errors will be taken in very poor light by any professional organisation.

Whether you are typing out your resume, or sitting down to write a formal email, make sure that your language usage is correct. Appropriate use of capital letters and suitable spacing is also important.

While writing emails it is important to address the person you are writing to correctly, using Dr or Mr or Mrs or Prof without error. It is also important to give your full contact details at the end, while writing formal emails. The subject should also be well worded and precise.

Do not use language that you are unfamiliar with. Write impressively by using whatever vocabulary you have, in an effective way.

While sending text messages, it is important to avoid using abbreviated words like 'd' for 'the' and 'n' for 'and'. Only when you are writing to close friends or family members can you indulge in such silliness!

We often tend to use small letters at the beginning of names while texting. Even this practice should be avoided. Young professionals who have been raised in the cell-phone era should be especially watchful! Only older people who find it difficult to use cell phones are at liberty to make such modifications to the generally acceptable norms. Their errors will be more readily forgiven than those made by younger people.Whatsapp messages are also in the same league, especially when invitations or formal bits of information are to be sent out. There is no excuse for using lazy and careless language on a group. It just gives the wrong impression about your personality.

Formal reports and papers prepared for official work have to be perfect in all respects. They cannot have any errors at all. These have to be properly titled and sub-titled. They have to be indented and spaced out correctly.

While signing a report or letter that has been typed by another person, you have to make sure that you have read it carefully and are sure of its contents. No one will ask later about who typed a letter with glaring errors. They will enquire only about who signed it!

The written word is expected to be exactly correct, and anything short of that is not acceptable from a good professional. Please avoid Common Indian Errors (a list of which is readily available online) to ensure that you do not fall prey to them.

Some common errors are the usage of words like 'advise' and 'advice' Also 'few' and 'a few'. Some people also say 'one of my friend' which is incorrect usage. It should be 'one of my friends'.

These are just some samples of words that need careful utillisation. Let us be meticulous when we use the written word, and let us stand out for being almost perfect in that regard!

What you need to do

- Practise the art of writing frequently by writing all kinds of reports, diaries and notes for yourself.
- Study the techniques that are used by great writers to present a point.
- Differentiate between various kinds of written communication. Know when to use formal language and where you can be somewhat casual.
- Do not use language that you are unfamiliar with. Write impressively by using whatever vocabulary you possess, in an effective way.

More Work Place Skills

Tip Number 11:

Goal-Setting and Goal-Getting

Life is a series of endeavours to reach short term and long term goals. We usually keep trying to attain something new, something that usually seems just out of reach. Goals are an integral part of our lives.

What's more, the goal posts of life keep shifting. Nothing is constant, and our goals are certainly not. We keep seeking newer pleasures, newer pastures and newer heights. Somehow we never reach a stage of total contentment, with the satiated feeling of having attained all the goals that we had sought to conquer.

While it is not wrong to keep aspiring for more and better in life, a feeling of being contented has also to be a part of your journey. Some people spend their entire life feeling that they have under-achieved and could have done much more!

A more fruitful way to live is by being able to celebrate and savour your successes, and move towards even more success from that state of mind.

When the Indian cricket team famously won the ICC cricket World Cup in 2011 with a magnificent performance under the leadership of MS Dhoni, hardly had they celebrated for 3 days, when they had to disperse to play for their IPL teams. The 1983 champions led by Kapil Dev, on the other hand, spent several weeks being feted throughout the land. Thewhole country participated in the joyous celebrations. Taking time out to savour your laurels is much more fulfilling than running after the next goal immediately.

Once you set a major goal for yourself, make sure you have time to savour it and share your joy at achieving it with your family and your friends.

The setting of goals should be realistic but it should also be challenging. What is life without a challenge or two? You have to work hard to reach heights which appear slightly more difficult than those you have hitherto scaled. But when that seemingly difficult goal is scored, the satisfaction which is attained is just phenomenal.

Goal setting should definitely receive the kind of attention from you that it deserves. Rashly planned or unrealistic goals whether they involve weight- loss or financial gains- are no fun at all! Goals should never be set in a hurry. You should think about them long and hard before commencing your pursuit of them.

Each goal that is identified has to be broadly in line with your overall aim and with the bigger goals of the organisation and your career. And goal attainment usually happens when you have laboured and slogged to reach your target. No substantial goal is reached without striving for it and sweating for it.

Attaining the goals you have set for yourself is also dependent on your killer instinct. Those who find life and its targets easy to handle, had better re-think their satisfaction levels. They are clearly capable of conquering much higher peaks!

What you need to do

- Goal setting has to be realistic and preferably aligned with the larger interests of the organisation. Make sure your goals are gettable.
- Unrealistic goals will only dampen spirits and curb enthusiasm. Do not chase them.
- Do not aim too high, or too wide! Your own capacity

and the circumstances you are faced with need to be kept in view at all times.

- It is necessary to dream big, but also to focus on achievable goals and plan your journey accordingly.

Tip Number 12:
Being a Team Player

Every individual has the opportunity to shine in life, provided some basics are in order. But not every individual is able to do so, and one of the reasons is a self centred approach.

What some people do not realise is that the more they focus only upon their own success, the lesser the chances of them achieving it. What needs to be understood by all young professionals is that their own growth is intrinsically linked to the growth of their organisation.

Just as a business organisation has to align its short term goals with overall objectives, so do its individual employees. The best scenario is when an employee is encouraged to align his or her personal career goals with the success of the organisation.

Thus a cricketer has to play for the team, an engineer-must work in coordination with his or her companions, and a surgeon has to ensure that his entire team is in sync with him in order to carry out successful surgeries.

Similarly, a Team Leader at an IT firm has to make sure that he is able to carry the team along with him. A junior software developer too has to ensure that her own individual brilliance does not for some reason undermine the work that all others are putting in.

Tina Kapoor, a young manager in the marketing department of a major telecom firm, had always been a very ambitious sort. She continually tried her level best to over-achieve her targets in order to receive extra financial rewards that the management was offering.

The problem was that she was so driven by her desire to outdo others that she often resorted to snatching the leads that colleagues had generated, and made them her own! Her charming personality and go-getter approach made her the darling of clients and she left others far behind in the race for targets. But predictably, she slipped badly on the popularity charts amongst her team mates.

It took a strong pep talk and lecturing by her boos to make her realise that her team skills were sorely lacking and that she needed to make corrections in her approach.

Some people will go to any lengths to further their own selfish cause at the cost of others in their group. The result of such machinations and even unethical behaviour is that the atmosphere becomes vitiated.

The organisation suffers and team effectiveness becomes non-existent.

Geoffrey Boycott, the famous England opening batsman was known to bat for long hours and get some of his partners run out! He never risked his own wicket. Even though he was a premier batsman of the team, he did not endear himself to the team or its followers by his often selfish approach. If the team needed quick runs before a declaration for example, he would just take singles here and there since he was approaching a century or another landmark!

There is no benefit in becoming unpopular with one's peers and friends in this manner. By being a team player, one can rise steadily on the ladder of success, and also generate a lot of goodwill.

What you need to know and do

- Being a team player means having the ability to align one's own growth with the growth of the larger entity.
- By sacrificing your own interests at times, in the interest

of the team, you actually gain in the long run.

- By helping team mates when necessary and supporting others when you can, you will achieve success as well as goodwill in life.

Tip Number 13:
Being Organised- Keeping To-Do Lists Handy

Many young people think that it is cool to be slightly 'unorganised' if not totally disorganised. The idea of maintaining a diary or a schedule organiser is something that they detest more than anything else.

The opposite habit, over-structured living, can become an obsession with many, but it is always better to err on the side of being organised than to risk forgetting dates and important rendezvous.

Other people somehow function by mastering the art of memorising all their tasks. If you fall in that category, good luck to you!

The rest of us really need to make sure we make a note of milestones which matter. There is no dearth of ways to do so nowadays. Smartphone calendars will pop up reminders just as efficiently as a secretary will!

The CEO of a fast growing advertising firm was sure of his personal organisation skills and prided himself for having the presence of mind to remember all his appointments without any aid. He also managed to remember names and faces very well. His team could not think of even one instance when their on-the-ball CEO had slipped up in any manner. He proudly stated to whoever would listen that he would never need a secretary either. He was just the Mr Perfect that everyone else aspired to be!

But fate willed that he would rue the fact that he had never used reminder aids. A meeting which was extremely important for his organisation never happened at all! The CEO was so sure that the said meeting was slated for a Friday that he did not bother to check his schedule. The result was that the potential client sent him a furious 'stinker' the previous evening! Apparently the meeting had been fixed for Thursday noon and not Friday noon.

There is just no harm in being reminded about something a number of times. In this fast paced era of hundreds of things happening at the same time, constant reminders are needed.

I know of a busy working couple who had to attend a wedding in the family. They were very sure that it was an evening bash. They reached home a little early from work and set out for the long drive to the venue once they had gotten ready. A casual glance at the invitation card let to a shriek from the lady though. The wedding ceremony and reception had concluded that afternoon with a sumptuous luncheon! They had no option but to turn around and dine out at an expensive restaurant- A place that matched with their dressed-up appearance.

An apology to the hosts via text message was all they could do to repair matters!

There is no harm in keeping a little note book in your pocket even in this technology driven era. I used to do that some years ago and found it a handy go-to notebook whenever I had to check something out about my schedule or a planned meeting.

And you don't want to miss a meeting with a boss do you? The repercussions would be far more serious than missing a wedding!

What you need to know and do

- Maintaining a To-Do List is a great idea.
- Being organised by using an electronic Google-enabled reminder system or through any other platform works well.

- Even an old style pocket diary and pencil will do, provided you can take out time to have a look at it once in a while!
- Reminders should be timed in a manner that you are comfortable with their timing.
- Organise your time as best as you can and you will become a much more effective professional.

Tip Number 14:
Preparing for Monday Mornings!

One of the assets that winners possess is the ability to plan for the near and not-so-near future. They are always prepared for any eventuality. Winners remain ahead of the game, ever ready for anything.

The rest of us have to work hard to keep pace with life and work. Sometimes we seem to be struggling to maintain our equilibrium in the face of each challenge that life throws at us, in rapid succession!

Planning ahead becomes highly improbable when we are not even able to catch up with current happenings and tasks. Yet we have to find a way to be prepared for more important milestones that lie ahead in our journey.

Monday mornings will always come. So will meetings and presentations. We will be asked to report or explain something by our bosses. We will be required to read some papers or do some research or prepare a PPT.

It is not that Monday mornings present the only challenging moments in one's career, but they signify those instances for which you simply have to be ready. Such moments of potential stress may arrive on any day of the week, at any time of the year.

At times one will know that they are coming, and one better be prepared. Sometimes they come without warning.

A sudden inspection by a senior functionary of the organisation, or a spur-of-the-moment decision by the boss to review the year's performance till date; If you are caught unawares, it is better to steel yourself and get down to the task without delay, and try not to panic.

Whether such trying moments come without warning or are pre-ordained, the winner will be he or she who is ever prepared. Being 'on the ball' and abreast of what is going on in one's organisation, means that you are taking close interest in your work. Only then will you be ever prepared for any eventuality.

Those who put off important work for next week will find it ever piling up. I remember the time when I was posted as the Director IT of Chandigarh, and I had additional charge of Public Relations Department as well as Tourism. It was impossible to find a moment of breathing space to plan ahead. But I took out time on Saturdays for 'thinking' work and preparing reports etc. Even though Saturdays were official holidays, the extra half day that I used to put in on Saturdays made me absolutely confident of being able to handle my work effectively.

I was thus well prepared not only for Monday mornings but also for unforeseen eventualities.

It is of course essential to adopt the habit of being punctual for this purpose. It is really a good habit to be present at the venue of an important meeting well in advance. Once you soak in the ambience of the place and settle in, you will find that half your nervousness has vanished.

I have seen many officers in my own career, and I too have been guilty of this on many occasions, arriving for a big meeting huffing and puffing, five minutes late, and molten at the stern gaze of the boss. Half their efficiency would vanish and they would end up fumbling throughout the meeting, just because they did not have a head start in the beginning.

"Well begun is half done", goes the old adage. There's no disputing the wisdom that it contains. Let us make it a point to prepare and plan well for each important occasion, and not be found wanting when it comes.

What you need to remember

- Be prepared for Monday mornings or any important occasion by planning ahead.
- Take time out from routine tasks to work on that little bit extra which helps you to prepare for big occasions.
- Arrive at the venue for an important meeting well in advance to soak in the atmosphere and settle in.
- Be punctual by habit and you won't be caught napping!

People Skills

Tip Number 15:

Learning Essential People-Skills

No matter what your core field of endeavour is, you will have to acquire an understanding of people skills in order to work smoothly and efficaciously. Those who possess a natural charm and an effortless ability to get along with others are truly blessed. But even they have to cultivate the right kinds of people-skills in order to become effective leaders.

Human and material resources are undoubtedly the two key pillars of any venture. Leadership is mainly about the ability to deploy these resources judiciously to achieve desired goals.

In particular, those who manage human resources well enough will always succeed in getting things done.

Leaders with refined people-skills will also earn enough goodwill to make their initiatives popular with their teams.

Akshita Sawhney worked for a firm that prided itself on maintaining excellent relationships with the external environment, especially with clients. She was new on the job but was learning fast and had impressed the management with a dynamic plan to boost sales. All went well until she got into a heated argument one day with a lady who was a long term client of the firm. The reason for the tiff was simply the fact that Akshita had not responded to the lady's calls a few times, mainly because she had been travelling over the weekend. But by not being able to assuage the angry client and by shouting back at her over the phone when they finally did speak, Akshita lost the plot, and nearly lost her job.

Dealing with unreasonable people is an art. Even if you are in the middle of something else or are not feeling well, you cannot afford to damage long term official or professional relationships. There is a way to handle them.

People-skills will enable you to placate people who lose their temper at you, and win over the hearts of those who are already amiable towards you. This does not mean that you have to be a 'softie' and let others steamroll you. It simply means that you do not lose your bearings unnecessarily and exhibit enough patience, according to the situation.

People-skills will also enable you to put yourself into the shoes of your teammates and others. You will be able to deal with them empathetically. You will be able to inspire your team to achieve great results. Goodwill will be your companion throughout your life.

Also important is the ability to deal with opposing personality types in your team according to their requirements. A shy introvert, a *silent type*, will have to be constantly encouraged whereas an aggressive go- getter, *a siren type,* will have to be monitored and controlled. This will enable you to get the best out of both types of personalities.

A high degree of emotional intelligence and its sister quality, people skills, will also enable you to know what to say, when, and in which company, as well as to avoid certain words when they should not be said. You will know that scolding someone in public is not the best idea, whereas praising someone in front of others certainly is!

As Deputy Commissioner of Panchkula I was often confronted with situations in which I had to speak to politicians or the media in the midst of the general public. By maintaining my cool and speaking calmly but firmly I was able to hold my own even in the face of pressures from people of all kinds!

People skills are the paramount skills needed for success in life and career. It is best to take time out to develop them early on in your journey.

What must you remember

- People are of varying types and it is up to you to understand them and deal with them according to their background and personality.
- In order to succeed as a professional leader, you will have to develop the art of knowing what to say, when and in what manner.
- By understanding others and maintaining empathy for them you will be able to generate the goodwill required to succeed as a leader.
- People are not machines. They need encouragement and tactful handling.
- Try and develop your people skills early on in your life.

Tip Number 16:
Maintaining Inter Personal Relations

Some people are able to maintain excellent inter personal relations with their colleagues at work. Others tend to completely fall out with some and enter into misunderstandings with others during the course of their careers. At times everyone's patience will be tested, especially when our colleagues remain the same for years, even decades. A scenario which necessitates long term working relationships is likely in a government job or even in a career-long tryst with a private company.

Seeing the same faces day in and day out for years on end can be very trying. And if wavelengths do not match or major disagreements and misunderstandings occur, animosity can increase to unbearable levels.

Familiarity breeds contempt, or at least it breeds tensions! Not much good is likely to come out of a group of employees if they are largely inimical to each other. Hatred at the work place can lead to highly unreasonable behaviour at the cost of efficiency and harmony.

Srinath and Mahesh were newcomers to a public sector undertaking and had joined recently. They had hit it off pretty well and used to meet along with their group for coffee breaks. Then one day Srinath said something jokingly about Mahesh that really pinched the latter. Mahesh would stutter while speaking and Srinath did not realise how embarrassing a matter it was for Mahesh. One remark made in jest and a mildly mocking imitation put paid to the bonhomie that the two had hitherto enjoyed. Srinath did apologise later to Mahesh but the damage had been done. And as they grew in the organisation, and gradually became senior pros, their dislike for each other increased in intensity. Srinath could not fathom why Mahesh should have taken such offence to his light- hearted comments, and Mahesh could not understand why Srinath had been so insensitive.

Years elapsed and the whole office knew of the tension between them. So much so that they were never bracketed together by the management in any major activity. Their skills and potential remained underutilised and their careers suffered to that extent.

Neither of them could really 'flower' and it was only because they worked for a PSU that they remained ensconced in their jobs. A private sector outfit may even have terminated their services.

Every professional has to realise very early in his or her career that the ego should not come in the way of progress and happiness. By forgiving team mates for remarks made in the heat of the moment, they would only help themselves. There is never any point in carrying grudges against anyone. Such thoughts and feelings are detrimental to one's own peace of mind, and also the health of the company for which one works. On the other hand, the habit of making insensitive remarks must be avoided at all costs.

Positive inter personal relations depend on factors like empathy for others, understanding that other people come from very different backgrounds, keeping small tussles under the carpet and effective or even effusive communication skills.

To appreciate the last point above, one can visualise a situation where the management never communicates its appreciation of employees, but simply gives them financial increments. Encouraging employees by writing well worded appreciation letters may work wonders. Inculcating in them a tendency to keep communicating effectively with each other really helps too.

Constant communication is the key to relationships of all kinds. Even a cursory pat on the back by the CEO or maybe a speech highlighting the contribution of untiring employees can really help to motivate the staff to perform even better.

What you need to remember

- Leaders across the board and at all levels need to understand that encouragement is the key to a smiling, happy, workforce.
- Colleagues need to spur each other on too, and neglect negativities that they notice, unless these are really bothersome. Even so, they need to forgive and forget when possible.
- Those in career jobs need to maintain at least cordiality with others, if not warmth, so that their work does not suffer.
- Maintaining good inter personal relations will enable you to do better in your career and your life at work will become much more pleasant.

Tip Number 17:
Handling Difficult Bosses!

One of the things about working for an organisation is the necessity of working under someone else's command. Until you scale the ladder and become a CEO yourself, you will have to be answerable for all your actions at work to someone or the other.

For that matter, even CEOs have the onerous task of handling a Board of Directors or a Chairman or an owner or someone else. There is no real independence when you are in the career mode and there is no way that you can get away with annoying your bosses repeatedly.

At times, hierarchical systems are so rigid that those senior in the organisation will always consider themselves to be superior in every way to their juniors. Unless a boss or a senior is a really good human being and is inclined to play the role of a mentor, juniors will have to pander to his moods many a time.

In some organisations this fact becomes even more inescapable. The chain of command is so inflexible and the pressures at work so heavy that the boss can virtually make or mar the life and career of a junior.

There are of course checks and balances which prevent misuse of authority and power, but these may not be effective unless the system is really well structured. So how do you maintain your calmness and equilibrium if your boss gets difficult or almost impossible in his behaviour? Supposing he badgers you continuously for months on end and makes your life hell by continuously being rude and tormenting you endlessly. What do you do, knowing fully well that you dare not complain?

There is no point in losing your cool with such a person. Why harm your career prospects by getting into a slanging match? Stay calm and maintain your composure as far as possible. The only way out is to find the right opportunity to speak directly to your difficult boss. You have to request him or her to give you 20 minutes to explain how much pressure you are under. And to explain how much better you would work if you were allowed to relax just a bit more, mentally.

Some bosses will see the reason in this. Others may not. But since you have made the effort to make your point, the boss will always be conscious of your pain points while dealing with you in future. And even if he or she has to write your annual appraisal which will boost or hamper your career growth, depending on how good or bad it is, you will be better off having voiced your opinion to him or her. Then, if matters get out of hand and you are compelled to approach the senior management because your boss does not seem to see reason and is hell bent on harming you, the management will take cognizance of the fact that you had already spoken to him. You will be able point out this fact and say that you have already requested your immediate boss, but to no avail.

I myself was regularly reprimanded, often unreasonably, by a boss I had. And one day he gave me a written warning which was totally uncalled for and which could have harmed my promotion prospects. I went to him with a copy of the warning and mentioned this to him. He took a long look at my face and heard me out. Then he took the sheet of paper from me and tore it apart!

"I regret my action. It was unfair. Now go back to work!' These were his words, and I left his room a little dazed but mighty pleased! Often it is the communication gap between you and your boss that inhibits better relations. If you do not voice your grievances to your boss and instead keep sharing them with your colleagues, sooner or later the boss will get to know of your oral complaints against him, and won't be very happy!

It is always better to take the direct approach. But of course, be mindful that you do not become a cry baby by going to the boss too regularly.

Overall you will find that bosses are reasonable people whose main aim is to get work out of you. But if someone is boorish in his behaviour or goes overboard, do not let that harassment continue. Take the initiative and voice your concerns!

What you need to remember

- Some bosses are difficult people, and act unreasonably at times. You have to be calm and not lose your cool with them.
- At the first opportunity, go and meet that boss and explain your difficulty to him or her. Request the boss to let you work in a tension free environment.
- If that does not work, you must approach the senior management at the right moment and explain to them that you have already requested your boss to amend his behaviour, but to no avail.

Tip Number 18:
Create Goodwill, Not just Popularity

There are some people who are always trying to gain popularity amongst their friends and colleagues. They make it an aim to rise upwards along the ladder of popularity. Others look down upon such tendencies and dismiss as 'populist' those who indulge in such conduct.

In today's era, I feel that being popular is surely a plus point in your career, but you must tone down your 'campaign' of becoming popular 'no matter what', if you have embarked on that.

Popularity and goodwill may have similar definitions, but they are distinct in nature. The popularity of an individual may be a fleeting and passing factor.

Popularity never remains on a high; it has to come down at some point or the other. It may be linked to temporary situations or certain actions that one has taken. Goodwill on the other hand is usually long lasting and does not succumb easily to fluctuations in fortune.

A school owned by my friend Michael's family suffered a legal setback and they lost the right to use the name that everyone had become familiar with. As a result, their popularity dwindled. They lost many students and new admissions declined in number.

But their goodwill in the community was such and their personal credibility so high that they recovered very quickly and despite having to use a totally different name for their school, they bounced back. They had accumulated good will in volumes after years of hard work and a righteous approach. They banked on it successfully to ride the rough tide and the sun shone once more upon them after a dark phase.

Goodwill is often accumulated effortlessly. But one can also work on it by being generally helpful and positive in dealing with others. A compassionate way of working, focussed on the welfare of others will always bring along buckets full of goodwill.

Self centred mindsets will never gain goodwill for their owners. People with such tendencies will fail to impress others even if they are very capable in their chosen field of endeavour. A large hearted and caring manner of working will always succeed effortlessly in winning hearts.

Popularity typically comes through overnight success or sporadic achievements. It is mercurial and may be a passing phase. But popularity sustained over a long period comes to rare people who possess genuine qualities of head and heart. Goodwill is the sum total of popular feelings that a person generates in others over a long period of time. You should strive to attain that.

Mr OP Singh, an old school teacher was standing at an air-port one day, years after his retirement, and was surprised to spot a young man with his family walking towards him and bowing reverentially. The young man introduced his wife and child to Mr Singh (and him to them) very proudly. He went on the recount tales from his school days and how inspired he had been by the persona of Mr Singh and his teachings. The young man also helped Mr Singh to check in and settle into his flight later.

The goodwill attained by the old teacher throughout his career, by virtue of his goodness and professional expertise was an invaluable asset for him. And the smile on his face said it all that day, when he realised that years of blood and toil had been worth it after all.

What you need to remember

- Goodwill is not something that comes with deliberate attempts at generating it.
- Instead it comes through being good at one's work and carrying empathy in one's heart for others.
- A cheerful persona is an asset too. A smiling and encouraging personality always attracts goodwill.
- You never know when such goodwill would come in handy in life. And the inner satisfaction that it brings is matchless.

Tip Number 19:

Networking - Being There When It Counts!

There is no substitute for being at the right place at the right time. Tonnes of talent within you will go waste if it does not find appropriate outlets for itself.

In the present era, being connected with the right circle of people is not only important, it is vital. Only by being a part of an organisation or group that really appreciates your worth will you be able to shine in life.

Enhancing your skills and capabilities to succeed in any field is highly essential, as you know. What you also must ensure is that you must raise your hand when it matters and you must be there, when it counts!

At times a career fillip comes unexpectedly, when you meet someone on a train and exchange cards, or when the man seated next to you on a plane eventually becomes your next employer!

There is a fine line between being an excellent networker, and being simply good. Some people under-do it, and others overdo it. Being too much in the face of those who seem important to you, all the time, is a bad idea. They will get put off very soon. Snehal was a young executive handling corporate Public Relations and she tried hard to connect with the media in the small town where she worked, so that her organisation could benefit. She would call up at least one reporter every day and try to meet him or her for coffee to become well acquainted with that person.

There was one particular lady who was a key journalist representing a major newspaper. But this lady was just not giving Snehal an appointment for their proposed coffee meet. She would put it off on one pretext or the other, or so it seemed to Snehal.

Finally Snehal called up that newspaper's editor, to request him to direct the lady reporter to meet her! This really annoyed the reporter, and though she met Snehal the very next day, she appeared cold and even rude in her attitude.

A very negative story about Snehal's organisation appeared under the by line of that reporter a few weeks later. She had obviously taken offence to the over eager persistence exhibited by Snehal. The reputation of her firm was in tatters and Snehal was fired, only because of her over enthusiasm.

This is an example of how over reaching can be counterproductive, how you must not push too hard at networking.

By being subtle and graceful in your approach, even when you are eager to network with a particular group of people, you will find more success.

Those who network also need to ensure that they have the innate quality within them that is needed for their work. There is no point tom-tomming something if it is not worth it. Inflated introductions often fall flat after a while!

Network building should be done for its own sake. It should not ideally be linked to sales targets or any such short term objectives.

I found during my own career in the Government that networking with people in general proved to be very helpful to me. Both in official and in personal matters I found that I was able to get things done just by making a phone call or visiting someone for a courtesy call. Being a people's person is always a good idea.

What you need to remember

- Adopt networking as a habit. Be willing to speak to new people and to introduce yourself.
- You never know when your own network may come in handy, for personal or official purposes.
- Networking need not be with a specific purpose. Just being a people's person will help you in life.
- Keep on networking throughout your life, and reap the benefits that accrue.
- Do not over do the networking habit though. Pushy attempts at networking may backfire.

Innovation and Change

Tip Number 20:

Innovating Endlessly - Standing Out With Ideas

'Innovation' is one of my three favourite 'I' words, along with 'Inspiration' and 'Integrity'. The innovator finds life more fulfilling and is able to make more of a mark in his or her care just by virtue of thinking and working differently.

Creative thinking leads to innovative results. He who spends his idle moments ideating and thinking of newer ways to get things done is the one who will blaze a trail of success in the world.

This of course does not mean that idle fantasising and endless dreaming will work. A worthwhile plan that is tangibly possible must be put into action, but wild and improbable ideas are not fruitful. It is important to keep reality in mind and constraints in view while planning an innovative alternative to a routine way of work.

One of the most innovative persons I have met is Abid Surti the Mumbai based cartoonist and writer. He is getting on in years now but is as sprightly and lively as a youngster. And what's more, he thinks like one. Always ready to laugh and always able to come up with new ideas and creative ways of working, Abid Surti is Mr Innovator.

Even in a staid and orderly kind of work-area like accounting, I have seen people innovating. Their ideas have resulted in efficacious use of time and more presentable reports. These are then easily understood even by those like me whose expertise in accounts is rather minimal!

The innovator is always ahead of the pack and always a winner. Even if his innovations fail, he will go on trying to make a mark by changing the way the game is being played.

A good way to find time for thinking out of the box is to set aside time for it on a Saturday or even mid week. Companies like Google and IBM encourage their employees to 'ideate'even during work hours. On the other hand some of life's best ideas often come in the shower or during a walk or on a long journey.

One of the ideas that I was able to successfully implement during my career in the government was a programme called C-TOSS (Chandigarh Training on Soft Skills) wherein specially engaged trainers would be deputed at schools and colleges to train students in soft skills. This led to greater employability options for them when they graduated. The dearth of soft skills in the youth has often been a complaint that the industry has had. Young people with reasonable technical skills just did not have the 'finished' personalities needed for them to be employable. C-TOSS definitely helped to bridge that gap.At times, even if the management is not supportive of an innovative proposal, it is worth bringing it up. Only the most dull and lacklustre managements will balk at an innovative approach to work.

Albert Einstein famously said, "We cannot solve our problems with the same thinking that we used when we created them!' While organisations may not always be responsible for creating the problems that they face, they should appreciate innovative ideas to resolve them.

Those with entrepreneurial ambitions will always have to adopt an innovative approach. It is not easy to establish a start-up that succeeds. While funding and support will also be key factors, it is certain that the ability to come up with a fresh idea will be a crucial deciding factor for success to be achieved.

By being a thinker and an innovator, you will always shine. Life will seem more fulfilling and enjoyable and you will never really grow old!

What you need to do

- Never accept age old ways of working as being irreplaceable. Always challenge yourself to come up with fresh ideas.
- When not actually busy at work, think about how you can contribute to your organisation's success, with new ideas.
- Set aside thinking time, each week, and put your thinking cap on!
- Once your idea is well formulated in your mind, put it across to the powers that be.
- As an entrepreneur you will always have to think and act innovatively to make a mark with your fledgling company.
- The ability to innovate is a quality that does not come easily, but can be cultivated by all.

Tip Number 21:
Adapting to Changing Times

We are forever living in an evolving world that can never remain the same. Can we then afford to rest on our laurels and stay where we are?

The fact is that change is the only constant. However young and up-to-date you may be, the chances are that you will have to adapt to newer ways of working and living as time progresses. There's no doubt that it is easier to pick up a new habit or a new fangled trend when you are in the prime of your youth. But as the years roll by and middle age approaches, you get established in particular ways of functioning.

When pager devices came and went, mobile phones became the norm. When mobile phones became smarter, those who could not adapt to the newest technology found themselves at a loss. How many of us actually use smart-phones to get weather updates, calendar reminders and fitness related statistics? Some of us do. But there are many features in smart phones which remain unutilised.

Most people use them for calls and social media and as cameras alone. There is no harm in that, but if you can adapt to the new features which technology provides, you can become more efficient in your daily routine.

Another example of changing times is the propensity for air travel. Have you become a smart air traveller or are you still lagging behind? Even train travel requires a degree of smartness these days. There are apps which can enable you to track where your train has reached and how late it is likely to be if it is delayed. Online check-ins and pre-ordered meals make life much easier for the busy air traveller. The idea is to save as much hassle and time as possible in this very fast paced world.

Apart from using technology for such aspects of life, it can also be used to order food, books and groceries. It can be used to read up material which might not otherwise be available. Checking out the Linkedin profile of someone you are to meet beforehand is a great idea and enables you to avoid the asking of unnecessary questions. Saving copies of all your important official and personal documents on your email id is an excellent habit too and increases the efficiency of your work as well as personal life.

Also important is to read up the latest developments in healthcare and lifestyle. Scientists and doctors keep coming up with new theories on fitness and health which are important to know; even if all of them cannot be taken at face value. If eating raw cabbage is a no-no at a restaurant, you must be aware of the reasons for this, and save yourself from serious infections.

Being aware of global happenings by keeping abreast of world news is also a habit that enhances your awareness, as well as confidence. And maybe someone across the world is innovating in a manner that can be replicated by you in your field of work.

Being cognizant of global best practices in your area of interest is a great way to stay ahead of the rest.

The latest trends in primary schooling can be a case in point. A small school in India would do well to adopt activities like celebrating grandparents' day for instance. Many schools in several countries have started doing so. With this little step your school will become more popular, if you run one, and the families of your students will be rather delighted!

The trick then is to remain receptive and alert to new ideas, and new ways of doing things. To be able to adapt yourself according to changing trends and to do so quickly will mean that success may come by more easily to you. Being resistant to change will never help.

What you need to remember

- Be aware and alert to global and societal trends as also changes in technology.
- Implement in your work and lifestyle those changes which will make your work-life and personal-life more liveable, efficient and enjoyable.
- Global best practises in your chosen field of endeavour can be replicated where possible by you.
- Being resistant to change will never help. Be adaptive and flexible!

Tip Number 22:
The Entrepreneurial Edge!

The percentage of young people who decide to plunge into the entrepreneurial world instead of seeking a job, is increasing day by day. And this is a healthy sign for the economy of the country. More business units will mean greater economic activity in all sectors.

The Government too has recently been urging the youth to become job givers instead of job seekers. But this is easier said than done. It is difficult for most young people to venture into a start up, to beat the risk involved and not only survive but also flourish enough to create jobs in the process.

An entrepreneur foregoes the option of serving a bank or a government or corporate organisation when he launches a small venture of his own. He has to be bold and confident in order to do so.

Let us consider the case of a Mumbai based young lady, Malti Rai, who is a commerce graduate. She might be under pressure from her family to settle down, get into a comfortable career, and get married. But she takes the bull by the horns and with a small loan or a couple of investing partners, launches an App-based online business with a fresh new idea.

She struggles through two years of rejections and heartbreaks since her venture finds few takers and success seems a far-fetched dream. Her parents keep pressurising her to 'be sensible' and apply for a permanent job. She takes long walks at the Marine Drive and thinks endlessly about what she should do in order to succeed. One evening, when Malti almost decides to throw in the towel, she encounters a senior lady walking beside her and they get talking.

They get on very well, the senior lady is impressed with her, and soon Malti has the requisite funding to scale up her fledgling business to a sustainable level.

Very soon, Malti's App finds popularity in the right segment of the local population. A section of the media carries a story on the young entrepreneur, and with fame comes further success. Her parents are delighted and her whole life has turned around for the better.

Being an entrepreneur means the ability to bide one's time through crises and setbacks, knowing fully well that one day the light at the end of the tunnel should be visible.

A certain amount of risk taking ability coupled with the support of the family is vital for a young entrepreneur. But even more important is to have an innovative idea as well as possible funding sources.

In fact of paramount importance is the 'idea' that can really excite people who are known as angel investors or institutional financial agencies.

The decisive edge that a dedicated, diligent and diehard approach will bring is the real clincher though. The novice entrepreneur will have to take failure in his or her stride and learn from it each time. In fact these days those who had failed start ups are seen as being more mature and experienced entrepreneurs than others.

From delivering used books at doorsteps to providing care givers for patients at home, some fresh ideas have impressed me recently. But what really sustains such ideas is a combination of luck and doggedness. Success is never assured, but comes more easily to people with these factors in their favour.

As an entrepreneur you never know when that handshake or business card exchange will lead to a breakthrough which you have been waiting for. Malti Rai found that x-factor just when she was about to give up.

The lesson? Keep at it!

What you need to remember

- Being an entrepreneur is not easy but it can prove to be worthwhile, provided you have the drive and never say die spirit.
- The x factor is worth waiting for. One day it will happen, even if you have been slogging for years, with no light in sight.
- A great idea coupled with family backing and a reasonable source of funding are the key.
- The entrepreneur has an edge over someone who is in a career job. He or she has the opportunity to really make things happen and can be a leader to the core.

Being a Winner

Tip Number 23:

The Winning Habit!

Some people spend their whole life being very dedicated and diligent, working extremely hard and almost achieving everything that they yearned for. The keyword that describes these under-achievers is 'almost'.

It takes something extra, a little more than most people can manage, to emerge a true winner. Much of it has to do with unending faith in one's ability. A lot of times it is the inner confidence which yields true success, but he who wavers at the last post, succumbs to doubt and fails to clinch that final victory which matters so much.

Let us take the case of cricketers Vinod Kambli and Sachin Tendulkar. Perhaps a lack of faith in himself was the reason why Kambli could not go beyond the initial forays into international cricket whereas his chum Tendulkar scaled unimaginable pinnacles of brilliance. Kambli was no less talented than Tendulkar, but perhaps lacked the temperament needed to succeed at the highest level. That made all the difference.

Milkha Singh came fourth in the Olympics and so did PT Usha. They are national icons and we revere them greatly. But had they been able to spur themselves on to put in that extra ounce of energy when it really mattered, perhaps they would have been gold, silver or bronze medallists for India in the1960s and 1980s respectively. India did not win an individual medal for several Olympics. Their success would have really lifted the morale of the country and inspired thousands of youth to try and follow suit.

That winning habit was in fact missing from most Indian sports contingents and individuals who competed at the international level. Some of it had to do with a culture of politeness as well as a legendary tendency towards hospitality. Winning at all costs and being extremely competitive were not really a part of the Indian ethos, for centuries.

The same docile and even apologetic Indian characteristics were noticed for decades in other fields of endeavour including professional work areas. Many Indians used to perform quite well in their careers but would somehow not really clinch the issue when it mattered.

It was when the IT boom came and Indians started travelling abroad more often as well as interacting with foreign professionals more regularly, that something clicked and Indians discovered an inner resolve which led them to become real achievers. Today, Indians are at the helm of affairs in many global companies and are able to hold their own in any scenario. They are often found at the top of the list in several types of fields- sports, business, academics, research and even entertainment. The winning habit comes more easily to them now.

Can you discover that ability within yourself to separate yourself from the also-rans and find that extra bit of passion to score a win? Of course this will depend on hard work and sincere efforts in any direction, but will also depend on your ability to convert neck to neck races into victories more often than not.

NR Narayanamurty, the co-founder of Infosys, never accepted defeat in the nascent days when the company was small and times were tough. Today Infosys is a global technology giant much admired and highly successful.

Edwin Moses won 107 consecutive international final races in the 400 metres hurdles category. Even after winning a hundred races, his winning habit obviously did not recede.

This habit is what the truly successful career person needs to cultivate within himself. And once that killer instinct is developed within, the trick is to not let it go. Ideally, one needs to keep winning, like Edwin Moses!

What you need to remember

- The ability to convert good situations into actual wins is a habit that can be developed.
- There are several people who under-achieve because they are unable to stay firm at the last post when it really matters.
- Keep your resolve and determination intact especially in crucial situations.
- Seek inspiration from great sportsmen or entrepreneurs who never accepted defeat.
- Once the winning habit is inculcated, do not let it go!

Life Skills

Calmness and Balance

Tip Number 24:

Positivity in the Blood

The one trait or characteristic which really defines a person is his or her positivity or lack of it. A naturally optimistic and buoyant personality is likely to attract more goodwill and make many more friends than a negatively inclined individual.

Positive thinking is a much under-rated but really important virtue to possess. So many people succumb to the habit of complaining about everything under the sun that it is rare nowadays to find a truly positive individual.

Tests and trials, even minor irritations, are bound to crop on in the journey called life. If we react with despondence and despair, wondering why such things keep happening, life will defeat us.

But if we ride the tide and bide our time, such dark moments will go away. If two types of people are presented with exactly the same situation in life, they will not respond in the same way. The positivity levels in them will determine how they deal with the situation. If one person can see the bright side of even a very difficult scenario and find a way forward, why can't another?

It all depends on the feeling within, on the attitude to life that we possess and go out with every day.If you are a team leader, then all the more so, positive thinking should be your goal. Leaders who possess and exhibit a gung-ho and cheerful approach even when circumstances are adverse are highly successful. It is imperative for a leader to instill confidence amongst the group and not let their collective enthusiasm ebb at any stage.

Virender Sehwag, the aggressive opening batsman on whom India relied for many years, to give them a flying start, exemplified the positive spirit. He would play in the same cavalier way, come what may. Some experts even called him reckless. But Sehwag was so successful that he is one of the only players in the world to have scored two triple centuries. He batted with positivity but not without method. He was very intelligent in the way he played. He knew which bowler to take on and in what manner. No one can score triple centuries and tons of international runs without being talented, organised and methodical as a batsman. But Sehwag exemplified the positive attitude that made him so successful.

Budding sportswoman Arunima Sinha lost both her legs in a train incident which ended her hopes of success in volleyball at the international level. But even that gruesome setback did not deter her. She began to train as a mountain climber even though she now had artificial legs. And she even scaled the highest peak in the world, Mount Everest!

Most people succumb to the habit of complaining and cribbing at some points in their lives. Little things irritate them and they lose their cool quite often. In the present era, with a fast paced life style and deadlines to meet at work for most people, for them to become edgy and negative is quite common.

But it is certain that happiness and success come to those who maintain their positive energy despite the odds being stacked against them. It is not easy but if Arunima Sinha can break the shackles of physical injury and scale magnificent heights, you and I can certainly do so in our everyday lives.

What you need to remember

- Giving in to negativity is easy, but leads us nowhere. Maintain that positive spirit even when things go wrong.
- Seek inspiration from great sportspersons or achievers who fought back despite the odds to become world champions.
- As a leader especially, you need to keep the chin up and not let others lose their enthusiasm even when adverse circumstances arise.
- Positive energy is a factor that should never be downplayed. Try and cultivate it at all times, throughout your life, and reap the benefits of happiness, joy and success!

Tip Number 25:
Being Fearless: Let Setbacks Strengthen You

Your success in life depends to a great extent on your ability to handle the little and big failures that will inevitably come your way. 'Life is a joyous battle of duty' said Paramahansa Yogananda, author of the Autobiography of a Yogi. Life can surely be joyous. It must be! But it is a battle all the time.

Feeling low for a long period after a 'failure' is a result of our inner make-up and attitude. Two people when faced with the same circumstances always react differently, at times vastly so. Success comes to those who overcome setbacks with fortitude and wake up the next morning with a 'can do' spirit.

The one who resolves to bounce back having learnt his lessons is the winner. Another individual may just buckle and collapse in the face of unrelenting pressure from negative forces that are bound to face us all, from time to time.

There is no such thing as a smooth life! Our lives are susceptible to knocks and setbacks, kicks and jolts.

Success and happiness come to those who gear themselves up to face upcoming obstacles, those who do not buckle in the face of pressure, and those who keep their cool when others around them have lost theirs!

A great example to follow is that of comeback sportspersons like Jimmy Connors. He won Wimbledon and the US Open at a tender age of 20. He failed to win the prized championship again for years, only to revive his fortunes and the quality of his game and win the big W once more at the age of 30, a ripe old age for a tennis player in those days.

I myself have felt low many a time during my journey. But I have somehow found the inner strength, each time with the grace of God, to come back and take on all challenges. Life is a topsy-turvy tryst. Let us try to keep smiling even in the face of real problems.

It is also important to have the right kind of company in such a situation. Those who believe in you will always encourage your efforts to stand tall. Do not spend time with those who are cynical by nature and are ever critical of life and its experiences. Jitesh, a Mumbai based young MBA was in the throes of a personal crisis. He had been laid off by his company and his fiancee had left him. He went into severe depression and spent many weeks lying on his bed and staring morosely at the ceiling.

But one morning he prayed mightily. He got up and gritted his teeth. He somehow found the will power to take on life's challenges. Soon enough he was ensconsed in an even better job. A year later love bloomed in his heart for a colleague whom he was to marry shortly thereafter. Life looked up and he soared high, believing in himself and not letting difficulties douse the fire within him.

Being largely fearless and not worrying about this and that is a facet of your being that you must strive to develop. Always realise that even the worst possible scenario will not mean the end of the world for you. As long as you are alive and have faith in yourself and in God, you will be able to succeed. You only have to strengthen your belief.

What you need to Remember

- Smooth lives do not exist! The lows of life are opportunities to re-invent yourself.
- The never say die spirit comes in handy when competition is tough and challenging times face us. Take a few days to

strengthen your mind when faced with such situations, gear yourself up, and get-set-go once more!

- Watch inspiring videos and mix with the right kind of people who will spur you on. Not with those who are negative by nature.
- Cultivate faith in yourself and in God. Try to be as fearless as possible.

Tip Number 26: **Cheerfulness, not Irritability**

There's no denying the fact that cheerful people are more popular than irritable ones. Those who retain a generally sunny attitude and do not easily lose their cool, are more likely to enjoy their lives and earn the respect of others.

The key of course is the attitude that a person presents to the world at large. A smiling and buoyant persona will generate goodwill and positivity all around, whereas a habitually snappy person will irritate others too.

An unlikely example I can give you is of a maid named Gayatri who recently commenced working at our home. She has a really beaming expression at all times and greets everyone with zest and a broad smile. She is the epitome of positivity and keeps everyone in good humour without going overboard. To top that, she is extremely efficient in her work as well.

Cheerfulness is not understood well enough by the common human being. People tend to confuse it with frivolity and non-seriousness. But the fact remains that smiling more and generating smiles from others is a quality which matters. Even if others don't directly notice your cheerful approach to life, you will leave a calming impact upon them. They will want to meet you again and again. They will also speak highly of you behind your back. But apart from these benefits, being cheerful is innately satisfying and also good for your peace of mind as well as health!

Irritability, on the other hand, is easy to fall prey to. Being cheerful needs an effort. Being irritable needs none. You tend to succumb to being short tempered and snappy just because it is the done thing or just because you feel like it. Our moods often dictate our behaviour towards others, and it is not surprising that most people let themselves down by succumbing to a negative mood.

If you compare the personalities of politicians who appear on television channels during debates, you will find that most of them are reactive and short fused.

Perhaps it is their mandate to forcefully put across their party's point of view at every such debate. But you can also spot one or two very calm and collected people in the mix, those who put their point across emphatically but never lose their cool.

It is not easy to possess a generally smiling face coupled with the ability to pull mildly a colleague's leg and also the knack of relating a funny story at the right moment. But some people do combine all or some of these virtues and make for great team members. Team work is about getting along with the rest of the group and being cheerful will certainly ensure that.

Personal relationships also depend largely on each party's attitude and conduct. If one partner is jumpy, irritable and short tempered, no amount of cheerfulness from the other partner will work. Some amount of effort to stay positive and feel as well as exhibit happiness, has to be made by both. But a cheerful human being will attract more friends and is much more likely to be successful in personal relationships as well.

This is not to say that one must remain perfectly cheerful at all times, come what may. When a situation is testing or grave, one must handle it accordingly.

When someone is feeling morose or downcast, no amount of cheeriness will help. Only a patient listening ear is perhaps needed!

But it is also true that sometimes in a tense situation the pressure is eased by a genuinely funny comment. Once when I was posted as the Sub Divisional Magistrate of Kalka in the foothills, the police and I were on our way to arrest someone who was responsible for blocking the national highway. The night was dark and the mood solemn. Just then I discovered a switch in the jeep which I pressed on impulse and a popular Hindi film song began blaring suddenly! Everyone in the jeep, cops and all, chuckled immediately and the stress of the situation suddenly vanished!

What you need to remember

- Being naturally cheerful will make you a very popular person in your life and career.
- Irritability is much easier to slip into, than cheerfulness, for which you have to make an effort at times. Watch your moods!
- Team members who are cheerful are liked by the whole group and stand out with their attitude.
- Real life situations in relationships as well as work often test your mood but by staying pleasantly positive you will always win the battle!

Tip Number 27:
Being Calmly Active and Actively Calm

In this world of demanding people, rushed lifestyles and technology-enabled chaos there is no dearth of restlessness. The quality of calmness is like an oasis in the desert. Very few people possess it, and even such people become testy when conditions are adverse, which they often can be.

Nobody can be perfectly calm and poised in all situations. Even while sitting quietly and meditating alone total calmness is not possible for the normal human being. At such times the breath flows gently and evenly. The mind does not dart about like a hare in the forest. The heartbeat too becomes moderately subdued. Yet, sundry thoughts keep coming to the mind , and calmness is a relative state, at best.

But even such a state of relative calmness is almost impossible to achieve when surrounded by people in a metro, or sitting at the workstation in office on a busy day. Even at a party or on a sightseeing vacation one is not really calm. One is enjoying the activity but the mind may be racing hither-thither!

So what can one do to achieve a reasonable state of calmness in every day life? Pramahansa Yogananda, author of the Autobiography of a Yogi, advised his followers to be 'calmly active and actively calm'. What he meant was that each of us can work towards being more calm despite leading active lives. The modern human being is a busy person and is active, physically or mentally. Even sedentary lives which computer operators or office goers lead are highlighted by deadlines to meet and targets to achieve.

What needs to be worked upon is the mind. The mind keeps worrying about this and that. Many people have their meals on the run and do not focus on their health. Those who spend time in the gym or outdoors find balanced calmness easier to achieve.

We must try and analyse our minds and decide which kinds of thoughts we can train the mind to avoid. Most of the time our minds wander here and there, as Psychology Today magazine found in a survey. By being actively calm, we actually monitor our calmness a few times during each day and bring our mind to obey our orders to stay calmer!

Another way to do this is to tell yourself that most of the things which you fret over are worthless. They are not important enough to keep your mind on tenterhooks.

If a friend said something that hurt you a year ago, why think of it now? Why is it still bothering you? Calmness cannot come to someone who lets little things bother him.

Our Mr Virender Sehwag is an example even for this topic. He would whistle Hindi film tunes while batting (between overs, perhaps!) He would hit a six when approaching a century. He even brought up his first triple hundred (he is only one of four batsmen ever to have scored two triple centuries in Test cricket) with a six! To remain calm at such crucial junctures when the spotlight is on you, and millions of people are expecting you to succeed, is a superb feat of calmness.

Calmness before or during an important meeting or interview will surely help you to perform better. There is no doubt that a restless frame of mind will lead to a diminished performance at any important stage of your life. Calmness will help you to outdo yourself!

By not fretting over trivial issues and by knowing that most problems of life actually resolve themselves over a period of time, you will become a calmer person.

If the pressure of expectation is hounding you, even then you can remain calm by telling yourself that success will surely come to you one day, if you keep working hard. And ultimately you are answerable only to yourself. Knowing this fact will bring a lot of calmness in itself!

What you need to remember

- Being calmly active and worrying less will lead to greater happiness and success in life.
- By being actively calm you will be able to monitor your mind and guide it towards remaining calm even in the midst of hectic activity.
- Ultimately you are answerable to yourself. Do not let the pressure of expectation that others hold affect your calmness.
- Your performance on any important stage of life will be superior if your mind is calm.

Tip Number 28:
Balancing Your Life: Fanaticism Never helps

It is good to be 'driven' in life. To have the yearning to succeed, to pursue your goals with passion, to strive very hard to succeed in whatever your chosen field is. There is no denying the fact that dedication and devotion to one's larger goals are musts for them to be attained.

But becoming too involved in your work and driving yourself to the point of collapse is not the right approach. Many professionals burn themselves out by slogging so hard that their families suffer and their own health may take a beating.

The career graph of a young multimedia designer Rajbir Singh was rising so fast that he was on top of the world. He became a Team Leader very soon, then a Group Leader and was tipped to be the Chief Technical Officer of the company in a few years. But Rajbir was a workaholic. His wife Naina and young daughter hardly saw him all week. Even on a Sunday he would busy himself with his laptop and almost ignore his young family. He had no time for physical fitness or entertainment. The result was that he put on a lot of weight and his blood pressure rose above acceptable limits. Naina and he started quarrelling a lot and the young child's psychology was adversely impacted. She began lying about her home work and exams. Her teachers were unhappy with her and scolded her a lot. The child became a nervous wreck. Naina had to leave her own content writing career in order to focus upon the child.Rajbir and Naina were on the verge of separation when saner counsel prevailed and a well meaning friend counselled Rajbir to mend his ways. Once Rajbir had seen the light he shed more than half of his work compulsions, opted for a lower level position in the company and began spending quality time with Naina and their girl. Within a few months life was like a bed of roses. Vacations, outings, book clubs and sports became an integral part of their life together.

Their daughter became a much happier child and her performance at school steadily improved.

Balance is the key to a happy life. There is no post or title which is more important than the happiness of your loved ones. If you analyse your own life and find that you are not spending enough time with your children as they grow up, please take a bold decision and cut down on your work life, even at the cost of your career. What good are all the increments and bonuses if your family cannot spend happiness filled moments with you?

When a tennis player scurries across the court to reach the line of the ball, he or she has to get quickly into a balanced position to return the ball effectively. Very few players can play offbalance. Roger Federer is a prime example. But most of the time Federer ensures that he is beautifully balanced while stroking the ball with finesse on the court. And in real life too, Federer along with his wife and his two pairs of twins quite obviously spend a lot of family time together, even though he travels across the world.

Balance is the one word and one quality that should be paramount in your mind. Constantly ask yourself, are you going overboard in something? Are you losing out on one important part of life because of another? The physical, mental and spiritual aspects of life all have to be given our time and energy. Social compulsions and family matters have to be attended to as well. Personal finances and most importantly, the children's upbringing must take precedence over much of our work.

Doing well in life is a function of many factors. But if you are balanced in your approach and give enough time to all your priorities, you cannot fail!

What you need to remember

- Working extra hard with dedication is good for your career, whether as a professional or an entrepreneur, but you must be wary of burning yourself out too soon.
- Family and loved ones have to be given more importance than your work life. Quality times needs to be spent with your children as they grow up.
- Balance means taking care of all aspect of life- Physical, mental and spiritual well being as well as family, social and personal compulsions.

Smart Tips for Success

Tip Number 29:

Physical Fitness and Sports: Be Outdoors More

The need for physical fitness cannot be over emphasised. People who are lethargic and low on energy will find it tough to get through their careers with any level of satisfaction.

Unless a major ailment has unfortunately impaired a person's ability to function effectively, it is imperative that each individual picks up at least one outdoor sport. Table tennis and badminton are indoor sports but they too are perfect for attaining fitness and retaining it.

Sporting endeavour is a way of life for millions of people across the world. They wait eagerly for the moment when they will step on to the sporting arena and do their best to perform well. Their physical fitness is a by product of the enjoyment that they get out of playing a sport. For someone who is not a sportsperson it is very difficult to understand and appreciate the joy that simply being on the sports field can bring them.

Just the simple act of kicking an old football around in a village street would give a young urchin unending happiness.

What's more, the happy hormones or endorphins which are released as a result of playing a sport improve our health parameters significantly.

Let us take the case of the internationally renowned centenarian marathon runner, Fauja Singh, whom I have had the privilege of meeting a few times. When he spoke at Play Write, our exciting Sports Literature Festival, in Chandigarh, his energy belied his 106 year old frame. He ate only vegetables and had some milk. He spoke softly and slowly. But his gait was as sprightly as anyone and even more so than some youngsters in their 20s who looked sheepish as he overtook them while walking towards the hall. Fauja Singh apparently started walking really late, at the age of 6. He started running only in his eighties!

Physical fitness, it seems, is as much a factor of one's state of mind, as anything else. You can actually will yourself towards regular walking, jogging or playing active sports, at any age, even if you have never done so, ever before in your life.

A sport like soccer or cricket may be difficult to play every day, since many players are needed, but individual sports like tennis or badminton are equally enjoyable.

Simply by running around a neighbourhood park, or walking fast, even for 20 minutes a day, excellent health and fitness can be attained.

Long hours at a workstation or a desk coupled with synthetic, processed, food and lethargic habits can put paid to a young person's fitness levels. Exercise and physical activity are a must even if you're very busy.

I have seen people exercising on the train or the plane too, and I have done so myself as well! Where there is a will, there's a way.

Another way to retain health and fitness is to walk a lot in your home or workplace. There is no point using a lift for 3 floors when you have the time and energy to walk up and down. There is much to be gained by walking to the water cooler yourself and having a glass of water, instead of asking your helper boy to fetch one. Even these little habits of being active can change your whole life.

Even watching sports at a stadium or on the TV is a better idea than watching soap operas! If one has interest in sports, life becomes more enjoyable and exciting. There is always something to discuss with another sports lover. And you never know where that sports related discussion may lead to. Lifelong friendships and opportunities are often created by conversations related to sports!

What you need to remember

- Make at least one sport an integral part of your life. It will make your journey more interesting and fulfilling.
- Physical fitness does not require major investment in time and money. Simply by walking, jogging or playing a game like badminton you can stay very fit.
- Walk whenever you can. Avoid using the lift if possible. Climb the stairs.
- Take an interest in national as well as international sport. Even networking opportunities may result due to a shared interest in sports.

Tip Number 30:
Time Management- The Art of the Escape!

Our own hesitation is one of the main reasons why we spend hours each day on activities that do not lead us anywhere. Sometimes we have to break the mould and get out of the rut we are in. To think differently and be a little more disciplined is what we need if we are to manage our time better.

Several people whom I meet ask me how I personally manage to be involved productively in so many fields. My simple answer to them is, I know what all is important for me, and I give those activities most of my time!

We are often compelled by the opinions of others, and spend time on things that we ourselves do not care for. Thus when a child has to embark on a 'boring' social visit with her parents, the child cannot avoid it, but would rather have been playing with her dolls at home! She keeps asking her Mom, 'When will we go home?', only to get scolded repeatedly by her parent!

Grown-ups, however, are largely masters of their own time, but they don't act as if they are. They keep going for those time consuming social visits which they do not really want to. They remain present at meetings and parties for hours, often long after they could have gone home!

One of the foremost plus points that I have been able to inculcate in my own life, especially in recent years, is to 'escape' from time wasting compulsions. Some people may have frowned upon the fact that I simply made a quick appearance at their dinner event, or just marked my presence at a wedding. But a large number of them were happy that I came, and hardly noticed that I left early. We are all busy, or should be, with our own priorities, and leaving early from an event which is a social compulsion is alright!

By spending a few quality moments with the host of a social event, and not appearing to be in a hurry, one can make one's move, well before dinner is served, by simply stating that one has another engagement! And that engagement could be with the family at home. Dinner at home is healthier and more wholesome than most food which is 'catered to'. Plus we can then share quality time with the family, which should be one of life's top priorities.

Of course there are many occasions which call for our presence a little longer, and we must stay for lunch or dinner at such times, but these are rare.

Another good idea to improve your performance at work is to leave in the midst of long meeting at times. Even if you are noticed as one who often 'leaves early', it is a great move to miss one hour out of a two hour meeting, especially when your role is over, by making a valid excuse.

Of course this would depend on who is in the chair at that time and how difficult your boss is, but yes it works many a time. You can go to your own cabin and attend to your work rather than being stuck in a situation where you are not even allowed to look at your laptop or phone!

On many such occasions, a potentially unproductive hour can be turned into a most creative and productive one, by making a determined effort.

Time management also entails the ability to adapt. In this era of omnipresent electronic gadgetry it is possible to work,research, communicate or entertain anytime, anywhere. You can work on the go and then spend quality time reading, meditating or chatting with family at home.

Do not carry work home if you can avoid it. Leave it behind you when you reach home!

What you have to remember

- The ability to know what is truly more important and to get down to spending more time doing it!
- Unless there are compulsions that cannot be ignored, you have to be doing what you prefer, rather than what you have to, most of the time!
- At social events, don't over stay. Make your excuses and leave when you can.
- Don't spend most of your work hours in unproductive meetings. Leave when you can and do some real work!

Tip Number 31:

Travelling Well-Not Feeling Groggy!

The modern professional has to travel a lot, mostly for work, but also for recreation and vacation. It is common for people to travel 2 hours one way for work every day in cities like Mumbai or New York, depending on which part of the metropolis they live in.

Touring jobs are also the norm these days. Video conferencing and Skype etc. have not really reduced the incidence of face to face official meetings. In fact business related travel has gone up manifold in the past few years. Airports and Railway Stations are buzzing, and the highways are choked with millions of people commuting for meetings or to work every day.

Travelling well has become essential for the modern professional. It is often required that he or she gears up for a road, rail or airplane journey in such a manner that he or she is in readiness for an important meeting immediately on arrival.

An executive who is into marketing a product or service nationwide would know the ropes when it comes to catching an early morning flight, meeting 2 or 3 different clients in any city and returning home late the same night. There is no excuse for arriving late to office the next day or feeling fatigued. The CEO will call a meeting at 10 am to demand details of the meetings held the previous day and their outcomes!

There are some who are natural travellers. Others struggle to get their act together on journeys. If you typically forget to carry your charger or a pen drive or something, you will always feel handicapped. The organised traveller will always keep a small bag ready with an extra kit and necessary items in it. If you are in a job where touring is frequent and sudden plans also come about at times, you will have to follow suit.

International travel has its own unique requirements. One has to be aware of these requirements, right down to the smallest detail. Not only the tickets and visa, but foreign exchange and insurance etc have to be taken care of. Even if your office takes care of such things, you will have to carry out some research on the locations you are planning to visit, their customs, their unique features and their logistical facets. If the airport is just 20 minutes from the city centre your hotel can be situated there. But if it is 90 minutes away, as is the case with many global cities, you will have to book a hotel nearer to the airport, and keep your flight timings in mind while doing so.

Also important is the ability to adapt to a new city or town. Mumbai residents are typically punctual and arrive in time for most meetings, despite the heavy traffic. Meetings in New Delhi may be delayed by up to one hour at times, even though the traffic there is no worse than Mumbai! By being smart! and keeping such factors in mind, you can travel very successfully and make your mark as an efficient professional very early in your career.

Airline staff will of course have to be even more adaptive to such needs. They will have to learn to live out of a suitcase and life for them will be about being able to enjoy their travel more than people from any other profession.

One of the examples of modern day careers that I like to often quote in my Talk sessions, is the case of a frequent traveller who wakes up in different cities, in various hotel rooms, all year long. He just does not know which place he is in when the alarm rings at 6 am, for him to catch his next flight. Recollection comes to him after a few moments and then he gears up for another day of travel!

What you have to remember

- Always be ready to travel efficiently, if your job requires you to do so.
- Be organised, while travelling within your country or abroad, by keeping the basics ready, so that you can travel at short notice.
- Do not forget to carry important accessories and be ready to attend and speak at an important meeting immediately after reaching a new city or town!

Tip Number 32:
Recreation and Enjoyment

One of the flavours of life that people often ignore is the chance and necessity to spend quality time with family and friends, just enjoying themselves.

Workaholics rarely find time to savour the fruits of their labour. They keep working day in and day out, forgetting to let their hair down once in a while. What use is a busy life that does not allow you to feel the happiness which is your birthright, by sharing light moments with people whom you are fond of?

Those who argue that they enjoy and love their work over and above everything else, have a valid point of view. But I can guarantee them that they will love their work even more by taking short breaks and completely switching off from the 'busyness' of work at regular intervals.

The great Greek philosopher, Socrates, famously said, "Beware the barrenness of a busy life!" And modern research indicates that many people really like the feeling of being extremely busy all the time. It usually gives them a false sense of power and achievement, it seems. When they realise that they have kept themselves inordinately busy for years without taking time out to 'chill' and relax, it is already too late. Time that has elapsed never comes back!

Actually the ability to enjoy life while striving hard for success in one's career, especially at a young age, comes easily to some, and never comes to others.

What is the point of not even being able to find some cheer and joy while the years pass by?

It does not take much to find moments of recreation even during a busy week. Even a game of table tennis at work or nearby will do. Otherwise a word game on a dictionary app. Also try dumb charades with office colleagues during lunch time!

Your children will be extremely happy if you come back from work and actually make the effort to chat with them, laugh with them, and play with them. A game of Scrabble or Cluedo or Ludo once in a while with your spouse is also a great idea.

Why should the modern professional have to don an ultra-serious professional garb all the time? There have to be times when you're having fun and a sense of feeling cheerful is the predominant feeling within you.

Work can also be made fun in various ways. Music is allowed in many offices nowadays. People can play music on their mobile phones or computer devices, and even watch sports at times, on a video screen.

Office parties and get-togethers are also a good idea, if not over done. At times parties can become dreary and drab, especially when compulsory to attend, due to office orders. But spending time with a group of friends over cups of coffee is a splendid way to laugh over your work related travails and exchange updates from your personal life!

What you need to remember

- Life is rolling by. Find time for yourself. Recreation and enjoyment should be a part of your weekly routine.
- By spending some time with friends and family regularly, playing something or just laughing and chatting, even a workaholic can make his or her life more enjoyable.
- Work can also be made more fun by introducing games during lunch hours and soft music even at the work station.

> Communication is the vital essence of all interactions between human beings. A smart, erudite and slick communicator will always be an instant success.

Tip Number 33: **Vacationing And Taking a Break**

During the hectic years of my career I would often be unable to take a break with the family and would eagerly wait for the first opportunity to do so. A whole year without a vacation is like an entire day without a breath of fresh air!

Countries like the UK and Kuwait mandate that everyone takes at least a month off from work every year. Those countries which do not make such holidays compulsory for their working population typically find that their national happiness index is rather low.

Some people really do not know how to go on a vacation or where. But they know how to sit in the sun and totally relax when they get a winter break. It is not important to actually go anywhere far away for a vacation to enjoy it. What is imperative is that you are able to switch yourself off from your work mode and truly calm down your mental faculties.

Those who carry their laptops with them to vacations and check their office mails on a beach are truly wonky! They are justified only if the boss has given them a vacation on the condition that they would reply to their mails once a day. (What a terrible boss!)

Even the act of spending hours on the smart phone while enjoying yourself at a destination like Goa, unless you're using it to click pictures of the sunset, is near sacrilege!

The Government allows its employees an annual or once-in-two-years Leave Travel Concession (LTC) which is often not availed. Employees often opt for extra salary instead of going on a vacation, if the Government so permits. The case is evidently the same with a large percentage of private sector executives if they are so allowed.

Why don't such people prefer to go on vacations? Why do

some people exhaust all their Casual Leaves and hardly ever take even a day off all year long? There is no doubt that they are very diligent workers. But what of their families? What of their own peace of mind? Is it not likely that their mind would benefit by sitting by the ocean or in a forest or on a hilltop. And what of the pure air that a holiday destination or even a village setting can provide compared to the air conditioned air of an office?

Is it not in the interest of their health and wellness that they take a break from their work environment at least twice a year?

The best time to take a vacation is of course when the children have holidays in their schools.. Twice a year at least, young school students do receive the benefit of such holidays. Vacations with family also help them to learn a lot by visiting new places during their growing years. If you have children, that is! Otherwise any time is fine.

If you're looking to avoid the crowds you can take your families to unique or lesser known destinations instead of 'popular' sites. Some people enjoy the rush-rush kind of vacation where they just keep scampering from one tourist spot to another, with not much time to sit calmly in one place. Others prefer to find a quiet secluded spot away from the hustling bustling world in order to recharge their batteries while reading a book or simply gazing into the blue skies.

Planning in advance for a vacation is highly essential too. Rude shocks can await families which do not research and plan at least a month in advance for the best fares and hotels etc. Nuances like which spots are appropriate for engaging a tourist guide and where they don't need one, are also to be examined beforehand.

The experienced and eager vacationer will learn over the

years to plan well and travel well with the family, and the entire clan will look forward to the next time when such an outing would take place. So make sure you live from vacation to vacation, while loving your work!

What you need to remember

- Vacations are essential for the busy professional and family.
- Switching off the mind from work related thoughts refreshes the brain cells and the mindset leading to greater efficiency at work on return from vacation.
- Families, especially children need vacations just as much as office goers do. Growing children learn whenever they travel to different places.
- Planning meticulously in advance is essential for a vacation to be enjoyed without hassle.

Tip Number 34:
Managing Personal Finances

There is a category of people, who are extremely diligent about their office work but very careless about their own paperwork. They spend years slogging at work, and doing very well. But when it comes to paying their insurance premiums, renewing their fixed deposits, or paying their children's fees, they are lethargic at best and forgetful at worst!

The amount of time such professionals spend on sorting out their personal finances, or keeping their personal papers in order, is minimal compared to the time they spend meticulously at work. If these brilliant persons were to spend even an hour a month on updating their personal databases and keeping their important personal documents in order, they would lead very organised lives.

It is important to check that you have filled in the nomination column in respect of your bank account(s) and lockers, if any. Also important are property and vehicle related papers, with their copies saved in physical as well as virtual form.

An easy way to do this is to mail a document to yourself and save it for a life time on your personal email id. A folder on your phone with the title, Important Documents, can also come in pretty handy.

You never know when you will need e copies of your Aadhar card, your driving licence, your passport or your PAN card. It is a great idea to keep them handy and easily retrievable in soft copy format instead of calling up your young school going kids to take a picture of any of these important documents when you need them urgently. Your fate in respect of an important application may well depend on their photography skills!

Brilliant IIM graduates Malini and Nidesh were so busy

with their entrepreneurial venture that they hardly had time for applying for the admission of their 4 year old to schools. Once they realised that they had better get going, it was too late for them to apply in many schools, and only a couple remained in the plausible list. Fortunately for them their child was admitted to a reasonably good school, not far from their home in Gurugram, but it was not really to their satisfaction.

They made amends when their second born was to be admitted a couple of years later, and applied everywhere! When she got admission to the best school in town, they were able to shift the older child to the same school under the sibling policy!

Being prepared for important landmarks in life is not only important, it is vital. You must ensure that you do not err on the side of carelessness when it comes to personal matters like these.

Even while carrying out online financial transactions and submitting important applications on the internet one has to be careful and set aside adequate time for the purpose. They would then avoid financial errors or other mistakes. Sometimes people are very careful with official matters and rather casual with personal ones like these.

Of course, one cannot spend office time handling personal work, unless there is no work pressure for the moment. Some people over do their personal tasks during work hours, others under-do them even at home!

The point is that in order to be a responsible citizen and even more importantly, an important member of your family, you will have to spend adequate time during your career to stay organised in terms of your personal finances and paperwork.

What you need to remember

- Be organised as far as your personal documents and finances are concerned.
- Always take out time, maybe once a week or once a month, to scan through your papers and place them in proper folders or e-folders.
- Always pay your children's fees on time and remember the deadlines as far as their school calendars are concerned!
- Do not let your family suffer because you did not organise your personal papers well enough as your career progressed.

Tip Number 35:
Avoiding Silly Mistakes In Life

Some of us are very adept at performing major tasks in life, but a bit clumsy with minor activities! I, myself, for instance often end up misplacing keys and parking receipts, thereby losing time in searching for them. If your family is waiting for you to pick them up and you cannot get out of a parking lot since you have misplaced the little parking slip, you will end up annoying them and feeling hassled yourself. Little mistakes like these often complicate our loves, and if they become a habit, then they can be extremely cumbersome.

Sometimes these mistakes come about because of our not focussing on the present moment. When we are continually distracted and not really mindful of what we are doing, we tend to become careless.

Absentmindedness comes to some people very early in life, and to some others, never. The latter variety of people is extremely careful about their possessions, their wallets, keys, mobile phones et al. But the former variety of people tends to lose any or all of these items at least a few times during their lifetimes.

Being clumsy is one thing, being forgetful or careless is another. But sometimes both these tendencies become a part of a person's make up and the result can be quite disastrous at times!

Inadvertently breaking expensive items at home or work is bad enough, if it becomes a habit. But if one also tends to lose papers that are important, or delete soft copies of documents which matter, then one really has to overcome such habits early in life.

Silly mistakes can often cost a family or an organisation a lot of money. There's a popular story which highlights this point. One individual carelessly miscalculated a bid that was to be offered by a company for some project. As a result, his company lost a million dollars. His boss duly summoned the erring employees the next day and our man expected to be thrown out of his job. But the reprieve he received was as shocking as it was amazing. 'We have invested a million dollars to train you, young man!' the boss told him, when asked if he would be fired. 'We would not like to waste such a large amount of money which we have spent to make you wiser! Now get back to work and make sure you never slip up again!'

Most bosses and organisations would not display such largesse of course. They may even institute criminal proceedings against a wrongdoer!

Road accidents too are mostly caused by reckless driving. There is no need to emphasise the point about serious accidents claiming lives. But even dents and scratches to your vehicle can cause you to spend hours at the garage getting it repaired, apart from the financial burden it causes. Very often we tend to forget traffic rules as well, or just cross a red light for the heck of it. The resultant chalaan or fine is not easily palatable though.

Basically the 'chalta hai' attitude has to be avoided, nay shunned, by the modern Indian professional. A cultural renaissance of sorts can be brought about in our country if young Indians start avoiding the tendency to be casual on the road and off it. Parking a two wheeler on the road since you were only planning to buy a loaf of bread, or taking a turn to the wrong side of the street in order to access a petrol pump, are some of the ways in which Indian motorists flout rules and make silly mistakes on the road.

Mistakes which one makes in life due to a casual or even callous attitude are totally avoidable, often damaging, and sometimes serious. Being focussed upon every action that you perform in your day to day life should make you almost perfect in this important aspect of life.

What do you need to remember

- Absentmindedness is a flaw which can be rectified if you focus your attention on each activity, big or small.
- Being mindful of your situation and the actions you are undertaking at a given time will make you almost 'mistake free'!
- Clumsiness can also be avoided if you are paying total attention to whatever you are doing at a given moment.
- Road travel and financial matters are some of the areas in which you just cannot afford silly mistakes.

Redefining your personality

Tip Number 36:

Emotional Intelligence is the Key

All human beings live and exist, or should, in a people's environment. Unless you have spent most of your life in the Amazon forest, taking pictures of rare bird species, you will usually be surrounded by people of all varieties.

Emotional Intelligence, according to my simple definition, is the ability to handle people and situations in a calm, balanced manner. Daniel Goleman, the authority on this subject, defines it as , "the ability to identify, assess, and control one's own emotions, the emotions of others, and that of groups". This definition is much in accordance with the thoughts of the creators of the term 'Emotional Intelligence', Peter Salavoy and John Mayer.

I have found in my years as an officer of the civil services that Emotional Intelligence is often sorely lacking even in the most intelligent of people. What use is the ability to solve complicated mathematical equations or to understand the theory of relativity with all its nuances, if you cannot speak kindly to a poor little girl who is begging at your car's window at a traffic light? What use are all the successes and achievements and accolades that you have accrued in your life, if you cannot speak calmly before the elderly members of your family?

Do we mostly know what to say, when to say it, before whom and in what manner? Do we more often than not behave as we should when it comes to handling sensitive situations of life? Since we are human, we will of course make mistakes once in a while based on the fact that we are provoked into saying something we should not have, or because we lose our temper.

Once in a while if we lose our temper, rarely, it is quite alright. Provided that even on such an occasion we do not overdo our tantrum or harm anyone in any way. Emotional

Intelligence also means the ability to check and control our own adverse reaction to a given situation, even if that situation displeases us.We simply have to retain some degree of control over our speech and actions if we are to succeed in any career. If we are to be proven as true leaders, we really have to be discerning as far as our own behavioural patterns are concerned.

Let us take the case of internationally renowned celebrities. If you read up the list of achievements of former World Champion Viswanathan Anand, you will realise that he has been as outstanding as anyone ever to play the game of chess, or any other game! But his calm, collected, yet confident demeanour makes him the ideal role model for any young person seeking to refine his personality. Emotional Intelligence of the very highest order is required if one is to stave of constant media glare and handle public adulation which comes in droves once you are a celebrity.

Sachin Tendulkar too has exhibited tremendous balance, not only while batting, but while conducting himself in public life. Both Anand and Tendulkar are perfect examples of a high level of Emotional Intelligence.

On the other hand, someone like Shane Warne, equally bril-liant, famous and celebrated, or even the magnificent Serena Williams, despite her astounding successes on the court, would not qualify as an ideal role model for young people.There is something else which a successful person needs in order to retain his or her composure in all circumstances. And that something else is Emotional Intelligence.

The really admirable CEOs or leaders of any variety consciously work on their inner qualities. They regularly analyse their own behaviour over a certain period of time, and they take corrective measures deliberately in order to iron out any deficiencies that they have perceived. They seek feedback from family and friends, even colleagues on how they responded to a particular crisis, and whether they could have done better. And when the difficult moment has gone, they still remain calm when they think of what had happened, even if someone had spoken in a harsh or sarcastic tone to them. There is no point in remaining balanced in the heat of such a moment if we are to lie awake for many nights in the days to come, feeling upset at what went on!

The moot point is that in order to be truly happy and successful, we must have a balanced, calm and positive way of thinking. We must be able to understand the pain of others when we need to. And we need to be examples for others simply by being individuals who inspire.

What we need to remember

- Emotional Intelligence is a must for us to be truly successful.
- We can cultivate those qualities which give us inner peace and happiness by working on them after having analysed our conduct at regular intervals.
- We have to be able to control our speech and behaviour in adverse situations.
- As leaders, we need to inspire by example, and not lead by force or authority.

Tip Number 37:
Anger Management: Staying cool!

Is an angry person normally feared or respected? Is someone who often loses his temper able to instil confidence in his team or does he get work done just by terrifying them?

In my workshops on Anger Management I often ask audiences as to how many times they tend to lose their cool per day? There are those who lose their temper 10 times a day; others, maybe once a week at most.

Human beings are temperamental at best, and will surely be provoked into losing their calmness at various points in life. But for some, the threshold of patience is high. These kinds of people are mostly unflappable and seldom ruffled. Their angry moments will be rare, if any. And they will come only if grave injustice is being meted out to someone they care for. But then, anyone would lose their temper in such situations, perhaps even a saint. Such instances are not really what we are discussing here.

The important thing for most of us to remember is that the more we lose our cool in everyday life, the more we will have to live a life of tensions and stresses. And so will the people around us. Every day life can be much more pleasant if we decide to not fret over avoidable issues. There are some people who will blow their top over a spoon that was not properly washed, or a bowl of soup that has too much salt in it. There are others who will not tolerate any interference in their work. Still others who will start shouting the moment they find that their car has been scratched by a passing vehicle.

These are the relatively minor problems, not major problems that commonly occur in life. Some of them are actually laughable, not worthy of even mild anger. But many of us will not be able to control our anger over them, and repeatedly so.

What is the way to remain less prone to such reactions

of anger which need not occur? The only way is to make yourself promise offline, when the angry moments are far away, that the next time you will not lose your cool over trivial or relatively trivial issues.

Doctors have told us time and again that anger and negativity harm the cells and functions of our bodies. Our health suffers due to frequent flare ups. The blood pressure surely shoots up!

A retired Brigadier from the army, whom I know well, tells us stories of just how much he used to terrorise his men while he was commanding a unit. He was truly feared and would make young men wet their pants with his ferocity. But once he retired, he started to think more deeply about life. He began to read spiritual books. He started meditating. Today he has become saint-like- humble, gentle, kind hearted and very soft spoken.

He regrets having been so aggressive and angry during his service days. He had obviously thought it to be a good idea at that time. But now he really regrets having spent his years in the army like that. He would gladly re-live that period by being as good at his work as he was, but with a much more amiable demeanour.

Anger really is our enemy. Nothing at all can be gained from it. The way to be is to be kind but firm!

What you need to remember

- Anger is totally counter-productive. No benefit can be gained by being an angry person.

- Certain issues which make us angry are not worth it at all. You must avoid losing your temper as much as possible

- Our physical health suffers too, if we are anger- prone.

- Being a firm, no-nonsense, person is much needed, but being firm does not need you to lose your temper, ever!

Tip Number 38:
Building up Your Leadership Qualities

Are leaders born or made? This timeless query may never be resolved by mankind. But there is clearly much to be said about working at your leadership skills. Even if you were not born with traits, habits and qualities which a leader should possess, you can cultivate many of them.

A few pointers here would help you to identify which of these you lack and need to build up. And this building up process does not take place in a week or even a month, but over several years.

Firstly, one can really work upon one's mindset. If you are a worrier, then you can reduce the tendency to worry by deciding once and for all which worries are worth the worry! If you tend to fret over trivial matters then you need to bring them under control first. Some people keep wondering whether they have locked the front door, for example. They get up from bed even on a cold night and go and re-check the door. Never have they found it unlocked! Try leaving the door open one night and see if anyone walks in! This idea may sound a bit drastic, but it might work. Half our worries can be gotten over with by letting the worst happen and then realising that it wasn't as bad as we had feared. Leaders cannot afford to have a worrying mindset at all.

Secondly, there has to be a certain amount of peppiness and joy in the heart. The French call it *'joie de vivre'*. An attitude that makes you simply love life. And for no reason at all you could find yourself smiling, or whistling, or even singing. Most people become like this when they have found love. But those who love life itself have reason to smile at every moment, without reason. This kind of attitude may seem too idealistic and not practical. But a spring in the step and an enthusiastic approach will only come from a deep rooted feeling of wanting to accomplish something special and going after it.

Thirdly, a leader will have to cultivate the ability to express himself or herself very well and communicate with others efficiently. There is no point in having a brilliant idea in the mind if it cannot be effectively shared with others. Implementation of such an idea requires team work more often than not. And clear-cut communication is the only way to ensure coordination within the team. Skilful written and oral communication is required of a leader. These qualities can and have to be cultivated.

Fourthly, leadership qualities like calmness and balance have to be developed. They do not come easily.

Everyone has human failings and these become exaggerated under certain circumstances. Provocation comes in various forms and it is highly difficult to retain one's calmness in the face of a verbal barrage or a mischievous campaign. But leaders have to maintain a stoic exterior even if they are seething from within.

And if they are cool inside then it becomes all the more easy to do so.

Lastly, while there are several more qualities that leaders need, shunning jealousy, anger and overall negativity is vital. No one can be a leader with all kinds of hatred and petty dislikes ensconced in the mind.

There has to be a large hearted approach to leadership. Forgiveness and an ability to encourage others have to be practiced by the aspiring leader.

Tennis superstar Roger Federer seems so calm these days that it is difficult to imagine him being the tempestuous 20 year old who burst on to the world stage, 17 years ago. He has obviously worked hard on his mind, apart from becoming the world's most skilled player. He is a true leader.

Most of us have to achieve smaller levels of transformation, and can certainly do so!

Stan Dale famously said, "I've always been the opposite of paranoid, I operate as if everyone is part of a plot to enhance my well-being!"

That perhaps best sums up the attitude that we have to imbibe, in order to be winning leaders!

What you need to do

- You can work upon those qualities which a leader should have but which you perhaps lack at present.
- A worry-free mindset and an enthusiastic approach help you to inspire others and lead well.
- Communication is the key to being able to convey your ideas to the team for effective implementation and coordination.
- Develop a large hearted approach to life where jealousy and anger have no role to play.

Creative Skills

Tip Number 39:

Social Skills and Conversation Skills

Human beings are essentially social and interactive by nature. The ability to smile and greet others, to carry out conversations, to encourage people, to love them and make them laugh- these are some of the abilities with which we are blessed.

In the current era, with its very fast paced lifestyle, it is difficult to maintain social niceties at the same levels as in previous eras. People are not able to spend enough time with each other. They need to be comforting each other when needed, just being there through ups and downs, and generally enjoying each other's company.

Conversely, technology has enabled people in different continents to keep in touch and wish each other a happy birthday instantaneously, but has reduced face to face interactions and even phone calls. Family groups on Whatsapp provide a platform for people to greet each other on significant occasions, by just posting a message that all can see, But a few years ago they would speak to each other on such occasions and may even have met when possible. I myself have not spoken to a few relatives whom I would call up now and then, since we are in 'silent' touch on Whatsapp and thus forego the opportunity to speak to each other.

The ability to carry out long conversations and genuinely show interest in a friend's work and life, is somewhat difficult these days. But you as a young professional have to make the effort to do just that. By being able to listen to others carefully without getting distracted by a smart phone or anything else, by sincerely and actually listening to them, you make them feel special. You also learn to focus on the present moment. And if you can do that in the nascent years of your career, while you are in your twenties, you will be able to do it even more in later years.

But those who develop the habit of not caring to listen

carefully to others as they speak are veering on the side of becoming unsocial individuals (though hopefully not anti-social!) Being a good listener is the key to being a good conversationalist. It is also a very healthy practice for the mind. The mind becomes calmer when we focus our attention on any one activity or object.

Focussing it on another human being is a good way to improve your own concentration as well as pay due attention to others.

Speaking clearly and with calmness is another good sign. If you pay calm attention to a younger person at a party and speak calmly to him or her in turn, you will really gain that person's admiration.

My point is not that we should seek to gain social brownie points by being attentive. We have to be able to carry out conversations and be good listeners if we have to grow in life.

Another important aspect of good conversation skills is the ability to encourage the other person to open up and speak about themselves. It is very convenient to try and dominate a conversation and speak about yourself and your priorities. What makes more sense is to be able to get the other person to talk in order to gain new insights from the conversation.

Boxer Ed Latimore said, "When two interesting persons have a great conversation, they completely forget to talk about themselves."

A great conversation entails exchange of ideas and knowledge as well as some humour and wit. Some people have a natural flair for that sort of thing and become very popular for the way they carry out conversations.

By being a socially active and pleasant personality you will become known and liked in your circles. If you maintain the right balance and do not over do the socialising bit, you will always do well.

What you have to remember

- You will do well to maintain good social skills and be socially active throughout your life.
- By being a good listener you will earn goodwill and will be able to understand aspects of life which are new to you with more insight.
- Conversation skills, with the ability to listen and speak calmly, are important skills to possess in today's fast paced world.

Tip Number 40:
Reading Voraciously!

Those who keep up the habit of reading in life always stand out easily. It is evident when you speak to someone at a conference or a social occasion or even at coffee, whether he or she reads or not.

The reading habit usually stays with the modern human being only till the teenage years. I speak to a lot of young people these days, and in conversations with them I realise that they had read some books during their school days, but stopped when they went to college. I can say with certainty that I would have been a better man with more knowledge and wisdom had I read more books than I have done in my life.

I too had stopped reading books after completing my educational journey and hardly read any for years.

Then one day I just decided that something is missing in life and I need to read all those books which I had been putting off for years. And having renewed my reading habit I have found myself feeling much more intellectually stimulated than I would have otherwise. Reading a mature global magazine like The Economist also gave me the much needed edge over others in my career. I would always know something about everything and could hold my own in any sort of discussion or debate.

So what are the kinds of books that you need to read? And in which language? I personally feel that any kind of book helps you to hone your personality in the growing years. Authors are usually wise and discerning people and very few of them write what can be termed as 'trash'.

Thus a Hindi or English novel would help you develop your language skills and make you think differently even if it is all about fun and games and romance at all.

On the other hand, an autobiography or a non-fictional self-help book would help you analyse your strengths and weaknesses and help you to improve yourself appreciably.

Even a murder mystery might not be a bad idea. Agatha Christie wrote some of the best ever mystery novels. Her books were based in European settings and her characters were always well defined and from varied fields. While reading her books as I was growing up, I would not only experience the thrill of a murder mystery plot, but I would also learn some amazing words and phrases, apart from increasing my general awareness.

I really improved my writing as well as speaking skills by reading Enid Blyton books in my childhood, and the humorous works of the peerless PG Wodehouse in later years.

The Autobiography of a Yogi by Paramahansa Yogananda is my all time favourite book, however. It has enhanced my life and my happiness levels multiple times by making me realise a little more about the true meaning of life. Reading great books by inspiring personalities will give you the motivation and verve to become an achiever yourself.

There is everything to be gained by adding that extra element to your personality with the help of great books. When you read the writings of a great man or woman you tune in much more to their ways of thinking and the true reasons for their greatness.

The newspapers and their editorials or featured columns too provide you with an opportunity to gain insight into important issues as well as to refine your vocabulary and expression. Magazines are almost on the way out but many are available in digital form and even global giants such as Time or the Economist have digital versions which are easily accessible to everyone.

Digital reading is also a good way to read on the move. Most people read while they are in transit or travelling these days. It is difficult to always be carrying a book around. You can download books easily on to your phone and read them on user friendly screens. Even in cramped spaces like the crowded compartments of Mumbai local trains, I have seen people read with unwavering concentration and poise!

A relationship with books is like a life-long love story that should never really end. Books can be your joy and succour in all phases of life. Go for them, caress them and depend on them to elevate your existence to much higher realms than would otherwise be possible!

What you need to do

- Develop the reading habit early in life. Books will be your lifelong friends.
- Read the classics and autobiographies of inspiring people but also read fiction/novels of all kinds.
- Editorials from leading newspapers and magazines such as the Economist or Time can be really useful in increasing your vocabulary as well as your awareness.
- Read on the move if you have to, by downloading books onto your hand phone.

Tip Number 41:

Creativity Brings Joy and Colour to Life

One of the things about life in India is the wide variety of opportunities for creative expression. For a young person the choices are unending. From sports of all kinds, to music of all states, to dance forms modern and traditional, to cooking dishes from across India and the globe, to photographing exotic looking people and fascinating natural surroundings, India presents its residents and visitors with a plethora of options for creative pursuits.

Add to the above activities like theatre, cinema, painting, art and craft, writing etc and you are almost spoilt for choice. Yes, these pursuits can be undertaken anywhere in the world, but in India with its mix of the traditional and the modern, the canvas of creativity is even broader, wider and deeper!

As a young professional on the move, it is very refreshing to be able to play the guitar on a Sunday or to photograph a lake early morning during an invigorating walk. The ability to do various kinds of different things is what really and truly matters since life becomes all the more appealing and enjoyable.

In my own life the writing habit has been a constant source of creative satisfaction. I had been a voracious reader in my student days and also used to write for the college magazine of the Regional Engineering College, now known as the National Institute of Technology, Kurukshetra. Having had an article published every year in the magazine called Vulcan, I felt rather chuffed at this fact. And the number of admirers I had grew in number too!

Boosted by my early successes as a writer, I started writing Middles in the Tribune and the Times of India after a few years of keeping very busy with my official work. Writing on Sundays gave me the creative outlet that I needed in order to energise my mind and go back to work afresh on Monday.

When the creative spirit is high, you can make not only your weekends zingy but also your regular work days.

There is every reason to spend an hour at a dance class after office hours if logistics allow you. Or a French class every alternate day. I was able to learn some French by spending a year and a half attending classes at Alliance Francaise. It is amazing how a little bit of effort in life to do something different will make your life more fulfilling.

And why restrict yourself to only those choices which I have listed out above. Think of something totally crazy or outlandish to do if you like. Spend your holidays preparing amateur videos on how to sing Punjabi folk songs! The sky is the limit for the creative spirit.

Letting your hair down like this really balances your life and you can go after your career related milestones with a much more calm and cool approach.

Someone like Dr SY Quraishi, former Chief Election Commissioner of India, exemplifies this approach to life. He plays the drums and is part of a band that plays music at friendly get-togethers. He is down to earth and amiable to the core when not engaged with official duties- quite a far-cry from chairing meetings and passing orders from a high pedestal. It was a pleasure to have him launch my first book, Move on Bunny, in 2011.

The idea is to retain your sanity and your enthusiasm for life by finding what makes your creative juices flow; and then finding time on a regular basis to follow that passion whenever possible in your life's journey.

What you need to remember

- Find out your creative talent and pursue it whenever possible even in the midst of busy days.
- Spend time on a Sunday or an off day writing, singing, dancing, clicking pictures, or doing whatever makes your heart feel joyous!
- Do not wait for a relatively less busy phase in your life to do such things, it may never come!
- Your mind and body will feel refreshed and recharged if you spend time on creative activities throughout your life.

Relationships Matter

Tip Number 42:

Choosing a Life Partner With Care

When you are young and ready to take on life, perhaps the most important decision to take is the choice of a life partner. There have been millions before you who have taken the right decision, actually billions. But many have made the wrong choice too. Incompatibility is one of the major reasons for young couples to separate from each other, often just months after getting married.

It is obvious that selecting the right person to marry has the strongest bearing on your life and times, The right individual can make life delightfully joyous. The wrong one can make it terribly unliveable.

In India it used to be said that we are to get married first and fall in love later. That was the era of arranged marriages of course, and it worked rather well for aeons, before the new fangled trend of individual choice becoming the norm. Falling in love should be a prerequisite to the choice of a marriage partner in such cases. But that is where some people err and others err disastrously.

Parents of young people of marriageable age often ask the couple to meet a few times and discover whether they 'like' each other or not. But these meetings are at best practically oriented and cannot really be a substitute for a friendship that turns into love as a natural process. Even if two people fall in love and then tell their parents there is no guarantee that the parents will agree. And there is no surety that the couple will still be in love after years.

But what needs to be done by each young person is to go with the heart and also the brain in such matters.Unless there is a basic level of mutual attraction and the nascent signs of love, a marriage is not likely to last. Gone are the days when the young lady would grin and bear discomforts that she had never bargained for while getting married. The level of tolerance that the women of India have exhibited over the centuries has been astounding. They have often suffered in silence, even in the face of physical assault and of course mental torture. But the modern woman is not ready to do so, and why should she be?

The risk involved in a modern marriage is thus only because of inappropriate behaviour and conduct. It is best that a young person therefore chooses a life partner on the basis of the human qualities that she or he observes rather than the outer adornments or position.

I often say that when a young couple are dating the young lady should notice how her suitor speaks to the waiters and the helpers. Is he a gentleman with them or only with respect to her? And the reverse is also true. The young man should be equally observant!

Time changes everyone and everything. People do not remain the same. But if the basic values are right, you cannot go wrong.

Marry someone therefore not for his or her looks, not even for his or her position in society, but for how good a human being he or she is. And it is easy to fall in love with someone who cares about animals and plants and of course the elderly. Such individuals rarely change for the worse over time. And if you just love the smile of your prospective life partner, you will probably not go wrong, but do check if the smile is genuine or artificial. It is difficult to be absolutely sure when it comes to choosing a life partner. The tug in your heart and your gut feel has a lot to do with it.

Leave the rest to the Almighty and your own basic goodness! You are not likely to go wrong then!

What you need to remember

- Choosing a life partner is the most important decision of your life, even more important than the career you choose.
- You must go with your heart as well as your brain. It has to be a mix of love and compatibility.
- If the signs are ominous from the beginning, and the person seems self centred or ill mannered especially with those from the lower echelons of the society, it is best to avoid such a liaison.
- Your own gut feel and your own basic goodness is not likely to go wrong!

Tip Number 43:
Being a Good Spouse

The most evident sign of a happy harmonious home is the behaviour that the children of the family exhibit. If a toddler repeatedly abuses, slaps or bites other children at pre-school, day after day, you can be sure that there is a certain degree of disharmony at home. On the other hand, a smiling cheerful young one will surely have a happy home to go back to.

When young professionals marry and become parents, they find that they have additional tasks to handle on a regular basis. They find additional emotional burdens being placed on their young shoulders. They discover that life is not a bed of roses even if they are shining in their fledgling careers and excelling at their profession.

Family life as an adult brings its own challenges and demands. A certain amount of maturity and patience is required to handle the varying pressures that begin to pile up as life goes on.

Gone at that stage are the carefree college days. All but gone are those moments of carelessness and even recklessness when friends would hang out till late hours and laugh endlessly. This is not to say that life's laughter subsides or dies down. Ideally it would go on increasing. But it is tempered by the realisation that there are responsibilities relating to the family and its well being which were not present before you grew up!

When married life comes along, there is a new paradigm at play, one which requires time and attention. Several young couples grow apart and even separate from each other very soon, only because they are unable to give each other the kind of loving care that should come naturally to those in love. Yes, the love or bonding which any two people share may not be strong enough to sustain the pressures of work life and domestic duties. But even if it is not, there is everything to be gained by being resilient and patient. Your partner is a human being too (hopefully!) and therefore will have some flaws which are usually discovered after getting married, and not while you are dating.

Niharika and Dhruv were madly in love and would meet every day after work. Their offices were in the same building. They spent many deliriously happy evenings together laughing and conversing about life and love. But once they had gotten married, tensions crept in to their lives. Both had been promoted by their companies and the pressure of work was immense. They were both ambitious individuals and did not like to compromise on their pursuit of excellence. The result was that they would return home late and hardly had time to talk to each other. There were few off days and even these were spent sleeping or working. Their love dissipated and they could no longer get along. The thought of having a child cropped up but they drifted apart before they could have one.

Some weeks in her parents' home made Niharika realise that she had taken Dhruv for granted and Dhruv's solitude made him miss her even more. The sage counsel of their parents and close friends made them come together with greater understanding than before and they had two children in the next 3 years. They made sure that they were able to maintain work life balance thereafter and gave their little ones quality time in their early years. The primary reason for the return of happiness in their lives was their willingness to be patient with each other. Their little bundles of joy multiplied the frequency and intensity of their smiles and laughter.

Those young couples who realise the need to walk half way towards their spouses even when the distance between them has grown, are the ones who are able to live in harmony together. An understanding heart will do wonders for a relationship.

What you need to remember

- Life is not a bed of roses and can become burdensome after marriage. An understanding approach will make it smooth and happy.
- Spending quality time with your spouse and realising that no one is perfect is the way to stay together.
- Patience and perseverance will be the key as life unfolds in the years after marriage.

Tip Number 44:
Parenting Skills

Your children will follow your example. They will not follow what you tell them.

Once you have ingrained the truth behind these words, you will be a parent par-excellence. Once you have children and they start going to pre-school a few years later, you will do well to spend as much time as possible with them.

Children pick up behaviour patterns and are influenced by the moods, language and tone of their parents in everyday life. As mentioned in the previous chapter they are greatly impacted by the environment at home. A cheerful home with lots of laughter and good vibes will mean that your children will grow up to be balanced and positive individuals.

It is impossible for a child to adopt healthy and constructive habits if his parents are not exhibiting the same. Those parents who lie in front of their children, cross red lights while driving, make excuses by the dozen and generally are short tempered, will find that their little ones will soon become advanced versions of themselves.

The reverse is true as well, of course. Good parenting means the ability to display good human qualities at all times, especially when the kids are around. The more a parent endeavours to remain calm and creative when the children are growing up, the more will be the likelihood of raising really good human beings with creative skills.

By spending time with their children on the play field, while reading books together, while watching wholesome movies, or solving jigsaw puzzles etc., parents will be able to win their children's hearts. They will be able to help build outstanding personalities of their young ones.

Parents often emphasise studies overly to their kids, at the cost of helping them to become all-rounders. Or they drive their children too hard in a series of activities all day long which leave the children little time for rest and playfulness.

Parenting requires effort. It requires planning. It needs time and care. It cannot be taken for granted! You will find that you have erred somewhere in your children's upbringing if they do not grow up to be the human beings that you wanted them to be. Outside influences are not as strong as parental influences, especially when children are very young.

It takes a lot of commitment and focus towards your children in their tiny and later teenage years to fulfil your duty as a parent. And there is no greater happiness than in enabling your child to be as good as any human being can be-full of positivity, compassion and calmness, cheerful to the hilt and full of character and courage.

Such qualities do not come without young people being inspired by their parents. By being role models for your children you will inspire them to follow your ideals.

When teenage comes and children become a little more irritable, short tempered or distant, preferring to spend times with their friends than with family, patience is the key virtue for parents to adopt. By losing your temper at growing youngsters, you will only alienate them and create a chasm between them and yourself which will be difficult to bridge.

The greatest gift you can give your kids is the gift of time spent with them, on walks, in games, on vacations, at meals, while doing nothing at all. Such moments are invaluable for a happy family and have a highly beneficial impact on a young child's mind.

When you realise that the most important investment of all is the love, care, and time that you give to your children in their growing years, you will be an ideal parent.

What you need to remember

- Parents are the most important influence on their children and their example is what the children follow, not so much what they are told to do.
- Spending quality time with the kids is the best way to help them imbibe the right values which they learn from noticing how their parents conduct themselves.
- Parenting requires planning and focus. It requires effort and care.
- By being good parents you will ensure that your children develop into balanced and positive human beings.

Tip Number 45:
Not Waiting for the Blue Ticks!

The advent of social media into our lives has brought in a lot of new factors into play. No one had ever heard of things like 'Likes' and "Blue Ticks"! They did not even exist. Such indicators of our social acceptance or relationship status are so important to many of us that they can influence our moods appreciably at times.

Some people actually live for the likes and the blue ticks. They spend so much time on Whatsapp that they need an extra few hours per day to get other things done. Over doing the social media bit is always going to result in heartaches and 'low' feelings. It is a rough tough world out there and people can be rather ruthless on social media channels like twitter, ensconced as they are in the comfort of their homes.

They post all kinds of things against sundry people and get away with such behaviour. And the sensitive user succumbs to such trolling by over reacting and feeling provoked enough to get into a slanging match which can only prove to be harmful.

The need for appreciation that the social media addict strongly feels is never ending. He or she can never be satisfied, even if a thousand likes are achieved on a post. The obsessive manner in which some people get into such modes can only be harmful.

Neelima was a busy executive with a financial services firm.She worked hard and had to be on the computer for several hours every day. But that screen time also allowed her the opportunity to chat with lots of her friends and upload posts many times every day. Her work was exacting but she had enough latitude to spend extra time on social media sites and whatsapp. Neelima became quite popular on Facebook but was unable to handle the downside of being ignored once in a while. She felt as though it was her right to have every single post of hers praised to the skies by her Facebook friends.

Her over activity proved to be counter- productive in fact. People started getting bored of the barrage of posts that she uploaded with irritating regularity. And she fell into depression due to which her work also suffered. It took a complete detox effort to get rid of her addiction to social media and her life certainly improved for the better thereafter.

At times personal relationships also become strained due to our unreasonable expectations on social media. Some people become livid if their partners or close friends have not responded to a message for a couple of hours. Such behaviour, according to psychologists, stems from the need for acceptance and recognition which many young people feel is linked to their popularity on social media.

Another aspect of this is the time of day that one indulges in social media. If one lies awake till 3 am expecting the party at the other end to respond till late into the night, one is bound to feel mental fatigue.

Those who do not get enough sleep because of social media obsessions also suffer health problems. Too much screen time is resulting in a lot of stress related illnesses as well.

The instant connectivity and ease of access that social media brings is also leading to greater jealousy among all sections of society. They view the posts of friends and colleagues with negative feelings at times, and rue the fact that they are not as hip and happening as them!

In summary, it would be a good idea to take the social media world with a pinch of salt. Too many expectations lead to disappointments and heartaches.

Best to spend some more time amid the trees and the breeze every day, with the phone firmly switched off!

What you need to remember

- Do not give too much weightage and time to the social media. Make use of its benefits but do not succumb to obsession with it.
- Avoid unreasonable expectations from the social media. Waiting for more ‘Likes’ is a fruitless exercise. You will never feel satisfied with such an attitude.
- Feelings of jealousy against others for having more ‘success’ on the social media are best avoided too.

The Bigger Picture of Life

Tip Number 46:

Integrity and Values never Let You Down

Thomas Jefferson said, "Honesty is the first chapter in the book of wisdom."

Integrity, values, truth and honesty are not mere words. They mean a way of life, a philosophy that endures, a challenge to fulfil amid varied pressures. And the truth is that those who follow the straight path never fail. They may feel low for a while, they may feel as if it is not worth it to be honest all the time, they may even feel that they are stupid to be so clean. But in the ultimate analysis, on the day of reckoning, they will feel content and happy that they did, despite all odds.

The gentleman's game of cricket has been sullied in recent years with a series of illegal activities. But such acts never go unnoticed in this era of television.

A cricketer who claims a catch which he knows he did not take cleanly, is soon found out. Steve Smith and David Warner were banned for a year for allowing the dishonest act of tampering with the ball on the cricket field. Those who have indulged in spot fixing or match fixing have found the law catching up with them sooner or later.

Several top cricketers like Sachin Tendulkar, Rahul Dravid, Anil Kumble, Virat Kohli, Shane Warne, Brett Lee, AB De Villiers, Jason Holder, Joe Root and Kane Williamson, as well as hundreds of others, can never be blamed for such tendencies. They have held the flag of probity and correctness aloft for decades. And this is also reflective of society and even the corporate world. There are millions of sincere, efficient and right thinking people out there

It may seem to the young professional who is struggling to make a mark in his or her career that success comes easily to those who take short cuts and even adopt unfair means in their career. But such success is not long lasting, nor does it result in permanent happiness. Somewhere down the line, such a person is caught out. He has to repent and suffer because of his deliberate attempts at climbing the ladder of success and prosperity by nefarious means.

The whole secret to success is to work tirelessly and persevere with an honest attitude. Even priceless virtues intelligence, capability and creativity come second to integrity and diligence.

Deepak and Nikhil were close friends who worked in the same division of an IT company. While Deepak was a slow and steady professional, who often missed his timelines but ultimately completed his tasks entirely to the satisfaction of his seniors. Nikhil was flamboyant and used to cut corners in order to be the first to complete his projects. All went well for the two of them and despite their differing styles they were doing rather well.

But Nikhil was a man in a hurry to become rich and successful. He began siphoning off work from the company's clients to his own self and started charging them a bit less than the official rates. He made a great deal of money this way for a while, since he was really sharp at his work. But one day his supervisor discovered to his horror that Nikhil was not being loyal to the company and was using his official position to benefit himself. He was thrown out soon thereafter and his career was in a shambles.

It is better to be like Deepak than tread a dangerous path like Nikhil. There is nothing to be gained by earning a fast buck dishonestly. Such deeds always recoil and prove to be the nemesis of those who indulge in them.

What you need to remember

- Honesty is still the best policy. Values like truth and integrity have not changed over the centuries. Even today they are the best qualities you can possess.
- Even more than intelligence and capability, you have to maintain dedication and honesty while going through the journey of life.
- Even if someone else seems to be enjoying a happy life despites being less than honest, you should stick to the straight path. He will suffer the consequences one day but you will lead a very happy life without mental burdens.

Tip Number 47:
The Art of the Pause

In each person's life there are several occasions when the need arises to relax, introspect and just pause. Life in the modern era is challenging to say the least.

People hurtle along through it without much time to think about larger ramifications. And before they realise it, time has flown and the impact of some developments cannot be undone any more.

A conscious effort to experience a pause amid the breakneck pace of a hectic life is a necessary breather which can recharge a human being. Without it one can easily burnout. Not much progress can be made by moving along mindlessly.

Whenever he delivered a speech, former Prime Minister Mr Atal Behari Vajpayee would pause several times. In fact his pauses were legendary. Momentarily he would seem to have forgotten his lines or would appear to be at a loss for words. But he would actually just be formulating the exact words which he needed, in his mind. And once the long pause was over, he would mouth his next lines so dramatically and impactfully that he would leave his audiences, friends and foes alike, spellbound and enthralled.

On several occasions in life, the pause is even more significant, even more necessary. Even a youngster of 23 years, who is eager to take a crucial decision about his career, cannot go on debating his options over and over again, unendingly.

He has to take a break and go for a jog or a long cycling trip in order to refresh his mind he may well find that the correct choice will come to him in a moment of inspiration while on a long walk by a lake!

The all important pause also re-energises the busy professional in the middle of a busy day. He or she will do well to take an unplanned break of ten minutes just when everyone else is getting into a frenzy. Unless there is a very pressing deadline a well timed pause may well freshen up the body and mind of the professional to enable him to give more than his best once he returns to work.

Forbes magazine, in a published article, advocates the pause as an effective away to relieve stress and avoid burnout. Putting everything on hold and just switching off completely might also be a good idea at times. Even a week's hiatus from work can really be beneficial to the overworked executive who has been overpowered by his workload and the targets he is supposed to achieve.

The thing to do is to assess your mindset periodically. If you find that you are becoming irritable, short tempered, and impatient, it may be because you have driven yourself hard.

Perspective and distance often provide vigour to a relationship as well. A boy and a girl, who are madly in love but have been arguing unnecessarily of late, might do well to decide to take a break from each other. They might just find later that this forced pause has done them a world of good and they are back to their lovey- dovey ways once more!

The sensible career oriented individual will recognise the need for pauses or breaks whenever he can take them. Human beings are not machines, and even machines need rebooting at times. There is everything to be said about respecting the fact that you need to refresh your mind and body every now and then.

What you need to remember

- Pauses are an important part of life. They refresh and recharge you.

- Those who are able to pause their work-mode every now and then will find that they feel happier and peppier when they return to work.

- Pauses can be taken every month, every week, or even during the middle of a busy day.

- Even a relationship may benefit if those involved take a break from each other for a few days!

Tip Number 48:
Meditation is the Most Meaningful Activity

Those who think that they will start meditating after retirement had better rethink that option. These days experts on health and wellness advocate that we should commence meditating at least for 10 minutes twice a day as early in life as possible. The mind becomes calmer and life becomes more livable.

I've been meditating for the last 12 years myself, and I have wished many a time that I had started much earlier in life. In a write up for my fortnightly column, Random Forays, in the Hindustan Times I wrote the following lines on this subject:

"What is the right age to begin meditation? Let's try and discover what enlightened people already know. The answer probably is that the right time to begin meditating is NOW. There is no point waiting for the day after tomorrow.
Thich Nhat Hanh says 'Meditation is not evasion; it is a serene encounter with reality.'
Those who think that meditation simply helps us to combat the trials and tribulations of the world, better think deeper. Yes, meditation is the most potent antidote to the caustic influences that this world of delusion has to offer, but it is verily also the route towards finding one's true self within."

Life in the present era is such that no one is able to find peace of mind very easily. Unless you live in a mountainous region far from the madding crowd, or in a distant village away from fast paced developmental activities, you will forever be bombarded by thoughts and kept busy with sundry goings on.

I myself started meditating at the age of 40, but wish I had done so much earlier in life. The battle of life would have become much easier had I taken time out to meditate twice a day from my early years.

Meditation brings inner peace to a much greater extent than through any other method, and it gives one the steadiness to combat the turbulences that life is sure to bring about from time to time.

Even during my busiest years, ever since then, I have been able to meditate regularly for about an hour each morning and evening, practising the Kriya Yoga path propounded by Paramahansa Yogananda. Whichever path you follow, and there are several of them, you must get down to the habit of meditation on a regular basis.

There is no greater sense of peace and calmness than the feeling of stillness which comes after a period of meditation. And people will then notice the same sense of calmness and an accompanying glow on your face during the busy hours of the day as well.

An article published in the Harvard Business Review quotes a research study that found multiple benefits of meditation accruing to CEOs who practice it.

Meditation, according to the study, increases emotional intelligence, builds resilience and even enhances creativity levels.

Youngsters who are just starting out on their career paths or those who are already in the thick of things, so to say, will do well to start practicing meditation twice a day, even if for just ten minutes at a time. Their ability to handle stress (and even the setbacks that come from time to time), would greatly increase as a result.

My own findings are that the best timings for meditation are early in the morning, just after one awakes, and late at night, just before sleeping. Saints will also suggest a similar pattern, if you read their writings. If you are unwilling to make the effort, you yourself will notice that something is amiss from your life.

Paramahansa Yogananda was such a strong advocate of the practice of meditation that he even said, "By the practice of meditation you will find that you are carrying within your heart a portable paradise."

Who would not want to carry a portable paradise within? Need I say more?

What you need to remember

- You need to start meditating regularly from early on in life. Meditation is not meant only for the retired!
- Even ten minutes of meditation at a time, morning and evening, would enable you to enhance your calmness and ability to handle stressful situations.
- CEOs who meditate have been proven to be more effective and successful in their careers. You must start making the effort, now!
- Follow any method that appeals to you, after carefully studying it.

Tip Number 49:
Seeing The Bigger Picture is Vital

The bigger picture of life is perhaps that perspective which enables one to avoid being short sighted and rash while taking decisions. The bigger picture also gives us a sense of life as a whole instead of viewing it in parts. Paramahansa Yogananda said that we must think in grand terms- "Eternity, Infinity!"

When we lose sight of the overall picture as we go about our daily activities then life becomes somewhat pathetic and meaningless. But if we consider ourselves as soldiers of the almighty, on the path towards victory under the guidance of the divine, we will never feel that way.

A young professional who looks at himself or herself in light of the national or global perspective, will feel inspired to try and achieve great heights. Successful global level Indian- origin CEOs like Satya Nadella and Sundar Pichai, must have ignited their will power to shine on the big stage at some point in their careers.

By aiming high and keeping the broader parameters of life and career in view all the time, one can actually rise much higher. Those who are worried only about increments and bonuses or instalments and bills will find that life passes by very quickly without much happening. Of course the mundane tasks of life have to be carried out to the fullest and attended to by everyone, but they should not bind one down.

Every Sunday or once a month one must sit down to see where life is headed, what is the direction that one is following and are there any course corrections needed? Such an analysis on a regular basis reflects maturity of thought. A thinker will be able to sort out his or her life much more easily, and iron out the chinks, when troubles arise, as they will.

Sometimes our ego prevents us from patching up with close

friends or relatives, even thought the origin of the problem may have been a trifling issue. Years pass before two people make up after a chasm is created between them due to a small misunderstanding, perhaps fuelled by mischievous persons. This is typical of many human beings who miss the point of life and are so narrow minded that they do not allow happiness to flow into their lives, because of their petty thinking.

Entrepreneur Tony Hsieh advises us as follows:

"Whatever you're thinking, think bigger!"

His advice may be more relevant to the context of an idea that leads to a successful business venture, but if you think of his words in the context of relationships, personal goals or a career, they make a lot of sense.

Why chase small shadows that do not exist and only clutter our minds? By emerging from these shadows and looking, in a manner of speaking, towards the sun, in all its glory, we are able to lead a larger and more meaningful life.

Mega-stars of the business world like Bill Gates, or Jeff Bezos, or Azim Premji, would never have been as successful as they have been without having envisioned themselves at the top of the ladder with huge empires to handle. And most top business magnates have also now started seeing the bigger picture in terms of helping others and doing their bit to alleviate the condition of the downtrodden. Gates and Premji are prime examples of such noble thinking.

There is a lot to learn from such inspiring figures. Large heartedness never did anyone harm. Abundance flows to those who are in the habit of giving!

Life is meant to end one day. It cannot be everlasting. If you view it in the larger context at all times, and shun petty level actions and thoughts, you will always shine on a bigger stage, and will be much admired and loved.

What you have to remember

- Always keep the bigger picture of life in mind, while going about your routine work. Never take steps of say things which are due to a short sighted attitude.
- If you think in grand terms and envision yourself as being a part of a larger, grander, global plan, you will be inspired to do more and better in life.
- Relationships which have gone sour can be set right if the parties involved show some large heartedness and see the bigger picture.
- Seek inspiration from the lives of those who have scaled the heights of the business world by virtue of being visionaries and by being kind hearted.

Tip Number 50:
Compassion for Others: Social Contributions

Everyone has a role in life, as a son or daughter, as a sibling, as a spouse or partner and usually as a parent too. Each of us also plays a work-related role, sometimes more than one, and contributes to the society as well as earns a livelihood in that way.

But what of others who are not as fortunate as us? What of the poor and the downtrodden, the illiterate and the destitute, the disabled and special human beings who cannot lead a normal life as we know it? All these sections of society need those who are more fortunate to support them in some manner. Through the setting up of a new NGO which takes up an activity like food for the poor or teaching the illiterate ones; or by being involved in an existing campaign to better the lot of the less fortunate ones, one can make a tangible contribution to society. Of course one can also donate sums of money as far as possible to well meaning organisations which are engaged in uplifting the condition of such persons in some way or the other.

The key is to start thinking in that way- a 'caring for others' way. And to not focus one's entire life towards self centred goals. The intangible benefits that come from helping others are immense and satisfying. There may be no material benefit in such activities. But the feeling of having contributed to the larger social good and having earned the gratitude of those who have been helped is far greater than any material benefit.

Your general goodwill can be enhanced in leaps and bounds through such noble actions. A lot of people miss the point when it comes to charity and social service. They think they are doing a favour to others. But in effect they are only playing their role in this world more constructively. And for the larger good. In fact it is for the fulfilment of the purpose of their own lives that such service is necessary.

The Tatas are known for their philanthropic ways in helping society. They have been doing so for decades. So have companies like Infosys and Wipro. Even if the Government had not made it mandatory for large companies to set aside a certain percentage of their profits for Corporate Social Responsibility (CSR) activities, such companies would have done so in large measure, of their own volition.

Individuals who are at the helm of successful organisations can also play a meaningful role for society. They should not think only of their personal success or well being. They should set aside time, effort and funds to enable their organisation to play a truly constructive role in society.

A plethora of youngsters are nowadays even making careers in the social sector. Even civil services aspirants are leaving the uncertain bandwagon of the competitive exams to opt for roles in multi lateral organisations or NGOs. Several such NGOs like Youth Alliance, Swasth Foundation, Teach for India and Goonj are enabling the youth to find a channel for their zest for service to the society.

It is extremely heartening to see many of them leaving lucrative multinational jobs and spending quality time in rural India. They have been able to collectively make a mark in ensuring meaningful interventions for the betterment of society in this way.

Everyone does not need to look for a career in the social sector of course. Wherever you are placed, in the government or in the corporate sector or if you are a self made professional, you can continually do your bit and serve the public at large in your own little ways.

From tree plantation to teaching the illiterate, and from

spending time with the elderly to joining save the-environment campaigns, there are many ways for you to be involved in the welfare of others and of the world. Do not hesitate and do not fail to find time for these noble causes!

What you need to remember

- Service to others is the noblest way to live.
- You do not need to be a full time social sector professional but can do your bit for society in little ways by spending time, money or effort, whenever possible, on a continual basis.
- Social sector careers are also becoming increasingly popular and meaningful avenues for young people to find a career.

Tip Number 51:
Mindfulness: Living in the present Moment

'Mindfulness' is a much discussed term these days. The need for it has never been as pressing as it is now.

Focussing in the present moment as opposed to letting the mind loiter around all the time, is highly beneficial to health, both mental and physical.

Those who practise mindfulness are reaping the benefits of simply controlling the mind a little and not letting it wander hither and tither. There is everything to be gained by not letting the mind dive into the past or scurry into the future, every now and then.

A student in a classroom, a young professional in training, an executive in a top level meeting- all these persons could be suffering from mind wandering habits. Their efficacy at work or study then becomes negligible. They are neither able to concentrate on the present task nor are they able to recall what was said, later.

At times there are reasons for our mind-wanderings.. Something troublesome may be bothering an individual. Or maybe he or she has fallen in love and can think of no one but the loved one! Even at such times, by analysing your thought process at the end of each day, you can direct your mind to focus on the task at hand rather than being continually distracted. One way to do this is to focus on the present moment

for five minutes at a time, by telling yourself that for the next five minutes you will not allow your mind to wander. And then repeat this exercise for the next five minutes, and then the next. Otherwise, several months may pass before you are able to pay adequate attention to your present task!

Gargi was a bright young management student who had all the makings of a highly successful professional and was likely to bag a job in a top level firm, her professors had told her. But something happened in her life that totally affected her performance at college. Her mother fell ill and was bed ridden. Her father had passed away a few years earlier. Gargi knew that their old maid was genuinely fond of their family and she would spend hours every day nursing her mother. Even so, Gargi kept worrying all day long about her mother and would call her every hour. So much so that her grades suffered and she was unable to make it to the selection rounds in the initial campus interviews.

Gargi became depressed and her life's pathway looked hazy and uncertain.

How could she have handled the situation in a better manner? She could have done so by increasing her faith in the genuine care that the maid was providing to her mother. The maid was a very good human being and should have been trusted implicitly by Gargi.

Moreover, Gargi's mother was stable now but her worrying nature made her think of nothing except the situation at home.

Later, when Gargi realised that instead of worrying she should concentrate on her career and getting a good job, she was able to unshackle herself from worries and distractions,and with a determined effort she bagged the final position that was available in the campus selections.

However great the reason for a distracted and wandering mind, it is imperative that an individual buckles down and uses his will power to shake them off.

Mindfulness can be practiced at any time of the day, for short durations, as earlier mentioned. And gradually the period of concentration can be enhanced and an individual can become much more successful by dedicating his whole energy to the task at hand.

Meditation and mindfulness are linked of course. Those who meditate morning and evening, even for ten minutes at a time, can focus much more easily on their work throughout the day.

Analysis of your day-long thoughts and their trends at the end of each day is also a good habit. You can catch your mind as it begins to wander the next day, by being determined to do so. Or else, before you know it, you will be half way across the world and day dreaming about acting in a Hollywood film!

Mindfulness and its regular practice can enable a professional to increase his or her efficacy at work and also improve relations at home!

What you need to remember

- Mindfulness is the practice of preventing your mind from wandering and engaging it in the present moment.
- For five minutes at a time you can direct your mind not to wander, and then repeat the exercise for the next five minutes and so on.
- By practising meditation morning and evening, your will remain more focussed throughout the day.
- Daily analysis of your thought trends will help you to control your mind better the next day, with a determined effort.

Tip Number 52:
Being Grateful: Loved Ones Matter the most!

Those people who prioritise work over family and breakneck momentum over calm family time may need to realign their thoughts sooner or later. Of all the various things that matter in life, spending quality time with your loved ones has got to be the most important one of all.

Many people spend their careers striving to make a mark and earn that extra increment or extra contract, without really realising the reason they should be doing all this. Years pass before they are able to pause and reflect on the fact that they have been running in the wrong direction!

Those career professionals who could not spend enough time with their children while they were growing up, realise much later that they missed an important part of life. And their children missed them when they needed them the most.

Fathers especially tend to be errant on this count, although in this era several working ladies are unable to spend time with their children as well.

The question that needs to be asked intermittently by everyone is, "Why am I doing all this?"And if the answer isthat you are doing it for the material welfare of the family and creative satisfaction, then too, you must ensure that you cut down on your 'busyness' and spend time at home more and more.

Tina Ghai was a busy banker and she was the head of Human Resources in the corporate office at Mumbai. Tina made sure that her children had the best of help at home through a reliable maid. She had a driver to pick and drop her kids to school as well as to tuitions etc later in the day. But months passed before she was able to herself sit down with them and understand their doubts, fears or worries as they grew up. Mamma was always busy for the kids. And Papa, Tony Ghai, was the busiest CEO in town. He was just inundated with work at all times, His phone was perpetually ringing and his laptop was seldom shut down.

The result was that when the children entered their teens, they adopted bad habits and had to be weaned away from them by the shocked parents carefully and painstakingly. Both Tina and Tony made an extra effort thereafter to undo the damage and spend hours every day with each other and their children, and sure enough, the young ones were soon back on track.

What is life about, after all? It is about love and happiness, is it not? And the simplicity of a family meal, with laughter and love permeating the occasion, cannot be matched by any other human experience.

No amount of wealth or riches can out do that experience. Then why keep running mindlessly? Let us try and spend quality moments with those who really matter in our lives. And let us be grateful for those people in our lives whom we really love. Let us not neglect the very ones whom we are living for.

That bigger picture of life referred to earlier in these pages definitely includes our parents, spouse and children. Siblings and best friends too. Let us not take them for granted in focussing upon our clients, bosses and those who seem to matter to our careers. Yes, they all have their place in your life, but give them as much importance as they merit. Not more.

For when you come back home to a chatterbox six year old and a very naughty four year old, with their smiling mother beaming at you, you will appreciate the meaning of life a little more.

So smile, love, share, care and skip along the journey of

life with happiness in your heart and cheerfulness in your demeanour. You will be more successful than any other person if you do so.

What you need to remember

- Life is meant to be spent loving and laughing, feeling grateful for your family and loved ones.
- Spend as much time as you can with your parents, spouse and children even during your busy years.
- Be thankful for all the blessings you have received and all the friends you have. Do not take them for granted.
- Happiness in your heart and cheerfulness in your demeanour mean true success.